"The Best Damn Internet Marketing Report Ever Written In The History Of The Universe!"

I0473551

By Eric Louviere

EARNINGS AND INCOME DISCLAIMER

No Earnings Projections, Promises Or Representations

You recognize and agree that the Author has made no implications, warranties, promises, suggestions, projections, representations or guarantees whatsoever to you about future prospects or earnings, or that you will will earn any money, with respect to your purchase of this ebook, and that the Author has not authorized any such projection, promise, or representation by others.

Any earnings or income statements, or any earnings or income examples, are only estimates of what we think you could earn. There is no assurance you will do as well as stated in any examples. If you rely upon any figures provided, you must accept the entire risk of not doing as well as the information provided. This applies whether the earnings or income examples are monetary in nature or pertain to advertising credits which may be earned (whether such credits are convertible to cash or not).

There is no assurance that any prior successes or past results as to earnings or income (whether monetary or advertising credits, whether convertible to cash or not) will apply, nor can any prior successes be used, as an indication of your future success or results from any of the information, content, or strategies. Any and all claims or representations as to income or earnings (whether monetary or advertising credits, whether convertible to cash or not) are not to be considered as "average earnings".

You understand that this ebook has not been available for purchase long enough to provide an accurate earnings history.

The Economy

The economy, both where you do business, and on a national and even worldwide scale, creates additional uncertainty and economic risk. An economic recession or depression might negatively affect your results.

Your Success Or Lack Of It

*Your success in using the information or strategies provided by this ebook and at the Website, depends on a variety of factors. The Author has no way of knowing how well you will do, as he does not know you, your background, your work ethic, your dedication, your motivation, your desire, or your business skills or practices. Therefore, he does **not** guarantee or imply that you will get rich, that you will do as well, or that you will have any earnings (whether monetary or advertising credits, whether convertible to cash or not), at all.*

Internet businesses and earnings derived therefrom, involve unknown risks and are not suitable for everyone. You may not rely on any information presented in the ebook or on the Website or otherwise provided by the Author, unless you do so with the knowledge and understanding that you can experience significant losses (including, but not limited to, the loss of any monies paid to purchase this ebook and/or any monies spent setting up, operating, and/or marketing, and further, that you may have no earnings at all (whether monetary or advertising credits, whether convertible to cash or not).

Forward-Looking Statements

Materials in this ebook or at the Website may contain information that includes or is based upon forward-looking statements within the meaning of the securities litigation reform act of 1995. Forward-looking statements give the Author's expectations or forecasts of future events. You can identify these statements by the fact that they do not relate strictly to historical or current facts. They use words such as "anticipate," "estimate," "expect," "project," "intend," "plan," "believe," and other words and terms of similar meaning in connection with a description of potential earnings or financial performance.

Any and all forward looking statements here or on any materials in the ebook or on the Website are intended to express an opinion of earnings potential. Many factors will be important in determining your actual results and no guarantees are made that you will achieve results similar to the Author or anybody else, in fact no guarantees are made that you will achieve any results from the Author's ideas and techniques in his materials.

Due Diligence

You are advised to do your own due diligence when it comes to making business decisions and should use caution and seek the advice of qualified professionals. You should check with your accountant, lawyer, or professional advisor, before acting on this or any information. You may not consider any examples, documents, or other content in this ebook or on the Website or otherwise provided by the Author to be the equivalent of legal advice. Nothing contained in this ebook, on the Website, or in any other materials available for sale or download on the Website provides legal advice in any way. You should consult with your own attorney on any legal questions you may have.

The Author assumes no responsibility for any losses or damages resulting from your use of any link, information, or opportunity contained in this ebook, at the Website, or within any other information disclosed by him in any form whatsoever.

Purchase Price

Although the Author believes the price is fair for the value that you receive, you understand and agree that the purchase price for this ebook has been arbitrarily set by him. This price bears no relationship to objective standards.

Testimonials & Examples

Testimonials and examples in this ebook and at the Website are exceptional results, do not reflect the typical purchaser's experience, don't apply to the average person and are not intended to represent or guarantee that anyone will achieve the same or similar results. Where specific income or earnings (whether monetary or advertising credits, whether convertible to cash or not), figures are used and attributed to a specific individual or business, that individual or business has earned that amount. There is no assurance that you will do as well using the same information or strategies. If you rely on the specific income or earnings figures used, you must accept all the risk of not doing as well. The described experiences are atypical. Your financial results are likely to differ from those described in the testimonials. You understand that this ebook has not been available for purchase long enough for the Author to determine what are typical financial results.

QUIT YOUR STUPID JOB!

Howdy!

My name is Eric Louviere and I'd like to welcome you to this book on quitting your job and working from home online. If you currently fight a boss, co-workers, traffic, a crappy paycheck... and feel like YOU LIFE is being sucked right out of you each and every day you go to that job, then this book is written just... for... YOU!

Dig in, relax and enjoy the ride. It will not be like anything you've ever read – or experienced – before! Let's get started.

It was a hot summer morning, humid, dusty, polluted and restless. The sky was hazy with smog when I awoke to the most annoying sound I've ever heard.

Buzz...

Buzz...

Buzz...

I reached over to the alarm clock and turned it off.

Forever!

That was June of 2006, and I have been a full time (no coat and tie wearing) work from home person, ever since!

I had found a vehicle... an avenue... a pathway... to making money from home on the Internet. I had done what most people dream of. I got to fire my boss.

BOSS.

It stands for double SOB spelled backwards.

I don't know about you, but all my bosses looked as miserable as I did, working a job they hated too, wishing something else could happen, that their destiny would be different and life would be somehow easier and more fulfilling.

Yes, even my bosses had that look upon their eye... of discouragement... of going through the motions... of just trying to make ends meet... of just forcing themselves to smile in the face of disappointment and ignore that beating fire inside them that says..."This blows! There's got to be a better way!"

"My job is kicking my ass"

"My boss is all over me right now"

"I might get fired or let go"

"God, I just hate my job!"

I'm certainly not saying YOU hate your job, maybe you love it. Maybe your boss is cool as the other side of the pillow. Maybe life is great and your job is secure and it's fun, rewarding, lucrative and special. Maybe you are lucky, like the rest of the 5% of the population who like their jobs.

I know I hated mine. All of them! It did not matter how nice and cozy any job was, I hated them all! Every single one of them sucked the ambition out of me and left me a dying robot with no hope of abundance.

But then again, I've always hated jobs. I've always strived for more and have always wanted more out of this short life we have on this planet.

I was that guy who had "business opportunity magazines" in my briefcase... who had "Get Rich" CD's in my car... and self improvement books all over my house.

I was that guy who joined MLM opportunities and would try and recruit you. I was that guy who would speak of "being rich" one day to my friends – who all grew tired of hearing my dream-speak.

I was the guy who everyone else looked at as... "He's setting himself up for big disappointment".

They did not read the same books. They did not focus in the same areas I did. They did not listen to those audios...

In fact, they made fun of those audios... and books... and dreams.

Their focus was on television, drinking, weekend trips, parties, their next week vacation, gossip, bills and family and friends. Every weekend, there was some invitation to some get-together.

The next day at work, everyone talked about the TV show that came on last night and what would happen next on the show. The Sopranos was big then, LOST, 24, and others I forget.

If you think about it, we mostly work 40 to 60 hours per week (or more if you include commuting)... and then there's the few hours each night of TV watching. Let's say 3 hours per night.

TIME, TIME, TIME...

A normal week, not including weekends:

- 50 hours of being at day job (including traffic)
- 15 hours of TV watching
- 10 hours of eating time
- 35 hours of sleep
- 2 hours of grocery shopping

Total: 112 hours

If you look at a five day work week, there is 24 hours in each day available and 24 times five days equals 120 hours. The above example is 112 hours. That only leaves 8 hours per week for "other".

Add in one night out for dinner at a restaurant (2 hours) and you're down to only 6 hours left. Add in shower time, take out the garbage time and cleaning your house time and paying your bills time and texting time and you're done. There's no time left for anything.

Of course there are variations, but we tend to fill up our time with stuff no matter what. Maybe you have 2 kids and don't watch as much TV. Maybe you work 70 hours per week, maybe you don't watch TV at all.

But, if we look at just **_time_** it's obvious why most people out there cannot escape the rat race. There's just no time to put towards something else?

It's about choices really. It's about choices as to where you put your focus and time.

Some people are ripped with muscles... are totally thin and healthy as can be. They work out five days per week, for two hours per day. They just don't watch as much TV.

Maybe they are obsessed with it and are pulled to working out and they just HAVE to do it. They MUST see results. Results are addictive.

Working out is where their focus is.

It's obvious to me, when I look at people and see that they put their focus on A) just reacting to life or B) on things that don't bring money.

"But Eric, exercise is important and life is important and I love TV shows, are you saying to focus all my time on money?"

No, but if you are mostly focused on "working out", then there's plenty of books on "working out" and this is not one of them.

Look, I'm not here to beat around the bush, I'm here to flat nail this down for you in a very direct manner. If you focus on other stuff, then it could take forever to quit your job.

It must be a primary focus. It must rank up there towards the top. You must put your heart and soul into it and you have to put in time. If you are looking for a magic button to buy where money spits out and all you have to do is put in 3 hours per week, then you are the "customer".

Are You A Customer
Or Are You The Merchant?

In the Internet Marketing community, you have thousands of people who want to be successful Internet Marketers. They eat this stuff up and they are rabid about this business.

But, you see them complaining about all sorts of things the "merchants" do. For example, you see tons of people complain about..."up-sells and down-sells" and they complain about videos that do not have the controls... and they complain about long salesletters... and they complain about email pitching... and they complain about pitch-fest seminars... and they complain about gurus... and they complain about prices... and they complain about launches... and they complain about guarantees... and they complain about hype... and they complain about getting phone calls or direct mail sent to them... and they complain about scarcity tactics... and they complain about unsubscribing... and they complain, and complain and complain about all things.............."Marketing".

Thousands of rabid Internet Marketers complain about marketing.

If you want to quit your job and be an Internet Marketer, then you need to become a merchant! You need to be the one selling stuff... not the one buying stuff.

Sure, we all buy stuff... I'm not saying that. I'm saying, be a seller mostly and a buyer secondary. Don't be a buyer primarily and a seller secondarily.

I'm saying sell stuff! Sell stuff now. Don't wait until you think you are ready, do it now. Sell stuff. Sell ebooks, sell audios, sell courses, sell PLR's, sell and sell and sell.

Sell all the time.

Always be selling.

Sell every day.

Every day, as a merchant, you should be doing something, every day, to drive income. Make sure, that every day, you do something that brings in money.

If you have a list, sell to that list.

If you pay for traffic, pay for it every day.

Do something every day to bring in money.

Get obsessed and addicted to cash flow. Put your focus on cash flow, not TV. Sleep less. Sacrifice your normal time that's dedicated to other things, and shift that time and focus to cash flow.

Don't spend all your time buying. That will only confuse you. All you need to make money online is this book you are reading right now. This has the answers. Focus on the methods in this book and do them. Follow them. Think for yourself and figure things out and stick with the task at hand.

Sell stuff.

Start with where you are right now, start with the knowledge you have right now. Start with the resources and assets you have right now. Become a seller. Sell stuff! Be a merchant, not a buyer. You are a seller, a marketer, not a customer.

Your income is going to derive from how much you sell. It's not going to derive from how much you buy. You have to change your focus and time.

Full time marketers (or those about to be full time soon)... focus their time and attention on "cash flow"... not distractions or buying stuff. They focus on selling stuff.

What can I sell NEXT?

What is something I can sell to my list today?

How can I get more traffic (leads) today to see my SALES-letter?

Is there a JV affiliate I can get to promote my "offer" to their lists?

You have to sell stuff. Sell more stuff. Get more reach. Get more traffic. Increase your conversions. The only way to make money is to sell stuff. If you are not selling stuff right now, then you are not a merchant, you are a student. You are a customer. You are not a marketer yet. You are not a full time marketer and you have not quit your job yet because you have not sold enough stuff.

Sell stuff.

Many people are afraid to sell. They hate being sold to, so they refrain from selling. They think they'll upset people by selling stuff. They are not aggressive enough to put themselves out there and sell stuff. They may have never been a salesperson before, or maybe they believe they are terrible at sales, and this transfers their thinking and self belief right on over here to the IM space. They don't sell stuff and they don't make money. Sell stuff!

Why are you not making money yet?

What Level Are You At?

- First Glance Level
- Student Level
- Newbie Level
- Intermediate Level
- Advanced Level
- Star Level

First Glance Level:

If you are at this level, then you are looking at Internet Marketing for the first time. It's all new to you. You just found yourself here and are not sure what this is even all about. It's all mumbo-jumbo to your right now.

You are just taking a glance at this business and have no clue what it's about or even the foggiest idea what to do next, or if this is even a real way to make money. You might not even believe this is real. You might think it's all a bunch of pie-in-the-sky thinking. You are not even a buyer yet.

If this is you, boy did you luck out by getting this book. And, yes, this is real. You should dedicate yourself to learning this business as much as possible for the next 30 to 90 days... and then SELL STUFF!

Student Level:

At this level, you are no longer looking at this at a glance, you're actually trying to learn it. You are starting to understand words like "copywriting" and "SEO" and know what a squeeze page is, and understand list building is critical... and you're just still learning stuff, starting to buy stuff more and more now... looking for people to follow... searching for answers... but not yet SELLING STUFF.

You might have tried selling something. I'd guess you spent no more than 4 hours on one specific thing you tried selling and you might have paid someone to set up a site for you by now. You wrote your own copy and there was not much copywriting to it. You might have bought a PLR product and tossed together some simple idea.

But, you needed traffic, so you wrote a few articles, maybe paid for some PPC or tried the traffic exchanges. After a few days, you got frustrated and looked for some other book or product to fill in the gap and give you a better chance at earning money.

But, you're still trying to learn and still seeking how this entire thing works. You still need to figure out how to get traffic. You are looking for help.

Newbie Level:

At this level, you understand the basics, the fundamentals of Internet Marketing, but you have not put it all together yet. At this level, you know you need traffic and you know how to set up sites and offers, and you've probably set up blogs and have submitted articles and dabbled in paid traffic and are just wondering where to focus exactly. You are a just a notch above student level, because you understand it better. You don't need to learn what "copywriting" is or what a squeeze page is, you know what it is but just need to put all the pieces together.

Intermediate Level:

Many are at this level in our industry. This is the level most people stop at though. This is the level most people reach and either A) quit or B) get stuck here for years.

This is that "hump" that most never get over. This is that breakthrough most never get past. This is where dreams die a slow and long death. Most will never get it though. Most will never pass this level and they will never understand that the problem they face... is right in front of them.

Most at this level will never realize that problem... the breakthrough... the reason they are failing... the answer they are looking for... the hump they need to get over... the problem is...

Them.

Yes, at the intermediate level, the problem is them. At this level, it's not the methods... it's not because of a lack of knowledge... it's not because of information or know how... it's because of them, their attitude and their self belief and their mindset. It's them.

I know it's hard. If this is you, it's a hard pill to swallow and it comes with a confusing – very confusing – shift in thinking that most will never get. Most will deny it, discount off what I'm saying here... ignore it... look down at it, perhaps look down at me and they'll debate this in their own head like a stubborn addiction of denial.

The truth:

Intermediate marketers who are not making money are not making money because of themselves, not because of a lack of methods... lack of knowledge... lack of resources... etc.

It's not the methods, it's them.

There is good news though. That can all be fixed and money can start coming in and jobs can be quit. The Intermediate marketer can breakthrough and get over that hump.

It starts with courage and focus.

Let's start with the levels of focus...

Dude, Where's Your Cash Flow?

Here are levels of focus in this business:

Student level:

Looks at information here and there, not serious at all, glancing at this business from a distance, has no clue, not sure if this is even real. Level of focus: 5 to 10%

Newbie Level:

Level of focus is 15% to 25%, but it's not focus on one thing, it's focus on all sorts of different things.

Intermediate Level:

50% to 60% focus, but it's not focus, it's time spent. It's time spent on all sorts of different things. The Intermediate might find he/she has spent 30 hours this week on the Internet, but none of it was laser focused on one thing. Most of the focus is all over the place. It's jumbled and there's a lack of "definite purpose".

This level earns some money here and there, maybe maxes out around $3,000 some months... gets gigs here and there, but is not earning enough consistently to quit jobs and rely on this income completely.

This is often the level where a marketer even starts building a name in the marketplace and people recognize the name. People start looking up to this person, but the person is not a full time marketer usually.

The intermediate level is a critical level. Some are fine with earning a little bit of money here and there and this business becomes a side business, something to do to earn some cash to pay for something or go on some trip or pay off some "all of a sudden" expense that pops up.

If the person is able to "want more" and become seriously focused on getting more, by escaping comfort zones and demanding more, then the next level is "advanced".

And the advanced level is where jobs are quit and big incomes are made.

However, the biggest obstacle standing in the way at the intermediate level tends to be "mindset" and "fears".

Listen to me now, your ability to eliminate or control these fears, will dictate your income from this level on up. You must suck it up and face these fears, diagnose they exist and defeat them.

The Fear Of Ridicule!

This one is a huge problem and it prevents people from getting to the advanced level and quitting jobs. At first glance, this fear may not seem all that big of a deal to you. Think again. It is like a sub-conscious disease that gets in your head, like a tick and buries itself there. Over time, it grows and grows and grows, paralyzing you from taking bold action.

At a certain point, that fear of ridicule (or criticism) prevents you from doing anything to generate cash flow. You start to second guess yourself and you start distracting yourself and talking yourself out of doing things.

If you do sell something, your customers' criticism is loud. If you sell to 100 people and 2 people hate your product, those 2 people crush your future action taking.

If a friend says something negative about your idea, you change your mind on the idea. If you have a new idea, you get excited at first, only to get disappointed when you look at the amount of work ahead of you with that idea.

You wonder if you'll be able to convert... or drive enough traffic... or if people will like it. You give a subpar effort on the sales letter or marketing of your new product or service.

You refrain from asking others to promote for you... or you get so paralyzed, you refrain from asking anyone anything at all. You start finding yourself being hasty, nervous, timid, easily persuaded, frustrated, down on yourself, complaining, casting blame everywhere but on yourself, blaming the gurus, getting jealous of others more fortunate, talking bad of others, lacking charm, bragging about past achievements, not expressing or standing up for yourself or your own opinions or ideas.

You become lazier and lazier, less motivated and less ambitious. Your energy levels decrease and you lack conviction for what you are doing or the task at hand. You second guess your decisions and let other dictate what you do to generate cash flow for yourself. You look to others to depend on them for your strength. You stop asserting yourself and you let others cripple your action.

If someone criticizes you or is rude (many are)... then it stops you flat in your tracks and you slow down all your decisions and action to a stand-still.

You start surrounding yourself with negative people, complainers and chastisers. You seek assurance as to why you might be failing and you throw rocks at those who are succeeding.

This fear steals the dreams right out of people. It's such a dominating fear, yet so unnoticed; it wins over time and crushes cash flow to nothing.

If something goes wrong and adversity shows its face, the fear of ridicule (or all fears) ignite into a blaze of excuses and "poor me". Many transition these fears into other outlets like "fears of bad health" and "fears of death" and fears of a lack of security and fears of being homeless or broke... fears of not being able to pay bills or put food on the table. "What will my wife think of me, what will my parents think of me, my friends and family??"

It's a real fear and it's one of the biggest barriers of all. And, the more passionate you are about wealth... the more debilitating this fear can be.

For me, I have had to battle this fear all my life. I can date back to my successes and see I had no fear of ridicule... and I can look back to my failures and see clearly now, I was full of fears.

When I'm confident, I'm bold and aggressive and I don't care what people think or how loud they criticize. If I'm down and out, feeling low and insecure, any stranger can say something of criticism to me, and I STOP AND SECOND GUESS.

When I look at marketing friends of mine, and see them selling their stuff aggressively, I see a confident person without a fear of being ridiculed. If someone does criticize them, they shrug it off and it's no big deal. They cast off that criticism like water off a duck.

Criticism is a given.

Here's how I defeat criticism:

I look for it! I try to get it. I welcome it. I want it! Bring it on!

Here's the key:

As long as I provide more value than the price tag is asking for, I'll be aggressive and sell the snot out of my offer! The ridicule is sure to come no matter what!

The more ridicule I get, the more people I'm reaching and the more "happy" customers I'm getting. For example, if I sell 100 units of something, I might get a 5% refund rate.

Out of those 100 customers, maybe 3 are rude and ridicule me. Heck, I'll probably get 5 more ridicule statements sent to me via email from people who did not even purchase the product, they are just complaining about "being marketed to".

"Can you remove me from your list, I'm sick of your garbage!"

"Go screw yourself and f@#$ off!"

"Piss off you scammer and spammer!"

These are people who joined my "marketing list". They are most likely suffering from an abundance of negative thoughts to act like that. Who knows, maybe their house is being foreclosed and they just lost their job that day. Who knows? Maybe they are just sick of being marketed to. People are resistant to sales attempts.

Anyway, if I sold 100 units, I might get 5 to 10 ridicule attempts on me. But, if I sold 1,000 units, then I might get 50 ridicule attempts on me. If I sold 3,000 units... well, I'd probably be immune to the ridicule because I had just sold 3,000 which is a lot at just about any price point!

If you are not being criticized, then you are just not selling enough products to enough people. You might make all your money with Adsense ads and never face criticism, but hopefully you're not just doing Adsense because of fear of ridicule.

Advanced Levels!

If you want to get to the advanced level and pass up the Intermediate level, then you are going to need to get your mindset right. It's a constant focus and requires long term dedication.

It takes effort and focus on your own mind. It takes being in control of your own mind. Take control of your mind, or it will take control of you. Fears will prevent you from moving forward and steal your dreams.

Ridicule is a given, embrace it. I've actually done things to ignite ridicule and controversy on purpose. It puts the spotlight on you and your offer. But, it has to be done the right way. There's a fine line where if you cross that line, the ridicule can kill your entire business.

In other words, treat people right, provide a ton of value for the price tag you are asking and be towards people how you'd like to be treated yourself.

If you cross that line and rip people off or stick it to them or scam them, then the ridicule could be the type of ridicule I'm not talking about. Sure, anyone can call your product a rip off or a piece of crap. But, if you are providing real value, then they are just chastising you. Their negative opinions are theirs, but not the fact.

There's a line you should not cross and that's to rip people off. You need to provide value.

You could be reading this book and thus far feel it is superior. You could be thinking that I'm helping you very much in this book. Others could have skimmed through it looking for some magic button, and then criticized it.

Others, they run and post glowing remarks online and give testimonials because I'm telling the truth here in this book and they respected that.

You never know who is reading this book. Maybe it's a student level person who does not even know this is real. Maybe it's a jaded intermediate level person who's pissed at the world. Maybe it's an advanced person who knows it all. Maybe it's a star.

Your mindset is critical and your ability to deal with ridicule is paramount to getting to the advanced level.

What Advanced Level People Focus On:

There are four main areas to making big money online from home, and these four main areas are where the advanced people can be found spending a majority of their time!

Here are the four main areas they focus on that the other levels don't:

- **Product creation**
- **Traffic**
- **Conversions**
- **Technical**

That's it. Everything can be grouped into those four categories and most of their time is spent there. Yes, they may go to a seminar, but why? They are going to improve or increase or take care of one of the above.

Other levels do not focus on these, or they may focus on one of them only. For example, maybe they just focus on technical... and spend their time working on their blog... never to get any traffic or conversions.

Most likely, they spend 90% of their time on everything BUT these four above. They spend their time learning or goofing off, or spinning their wheels, on forums, reading blogs, etc instead of focusing on the four above.

Advanced level marketers also have an advantage usually. They have something very compelling that is forcing them to focus on the four above. These advanced level people have something forcing them to be courageous and defeat their fears, and take bold action.

That compelling thing is... they have to in order to pay the bills and put food on the table. You see, most advanced level people are full time marketers and they are the bread winners.

They have a lot of bills to pay too. They have made a lot of money online and they have to take bold action and focus on the four above because if not, they don't earn money.

They are addicted to cash flow. They've felt the emotions of working for themselves and they know they have to get their tails in gear if they want to earn more or continue to live the lifestyle they are used to.

Most likely, they are the bread winner now. They don't depend on a wife or a husband to pay the bills... because their wife or husband probably quit his/her job already and maybe works in the business or does not work at all.

Intermediate people never get here, and sometimes it's BECAUSE they are depending on a significant other to pay the bills. That's called complacency and it's easy to NOT take action when someone is taking care of them.

I've seen this a ton of times. Wife makes good money, husband makes a little bit here and there with his Internet Marketing hobby. Parents pay the bills, so son is complacent and lazy and wastes time with distractions instead of focusing on the four main things:

- **Product creation**
- **Traffic**
- **Conversions**
- **Technical**

Advanced level people have no choice anymore really. I mean, they always have a choice, but there's a fire there now. There's a "work ethic" there now... and there's a "pulling" there now, just like that person who is addicted to working out. The muscle man feels bad... feels like crap... if he does not work out.

Same for the advanced level marketer...

You have to be compelled and have a burning desire to get from intermediate to "advanced". You have to be willing to change. Change your focus and change your self-belief. Change your actions and change your confidence. Change your reach, and change your aggressiveness! Change your effort and change your results. Demand more of yourself, and demand more of your cash flow. Want more, expect more and go get more!

Question: Where do you focus most of your time now?

If it's not on the four mentioned above, then it better be on your mindset. Everything else is a distraction. Sure, you got to spend time with the kids and all those kinds of things, but when you work, you need to work on one of these five:

- **Product creation**
- **Traffic**
- **Conversions**
- **Technical**

- **Mindset!**

Question: How much time do you realistically have each week to put into these above things?

I slept less. At my day job, I worked during my lunch hour. I worked on my business while I was at work too. I worked until late at night. I worked on the weekends. I worked on vacations. I took sick time to work on my business. Six months later, I turned off that alarm clock forever!

Specialized Knowledge:

Most people never get good at one thing. They spend their time on a lot of different things. For example, they get 10% good at traffic, conversions, product creation, etc.

They never get very good at one thing, like traffic. If you spend all your time focused on just one thing, like traffic, you'll be able to make six figures most likely.

It's the same with copywriting. If you spend all your time on copywriting, then you'll get so good at it, you should be able to make six figures with just copywriting.

Here are some areas you can get good at:

- Copywriting
- Driving traffic
- Product creation
- Technical
- Contacts (which is like traffic)

Unfortunately, most will continue to not get very good at any of the above and only get 10% good at all of them. 10% is not good enough and will never allow you to quit a job or earn six figures.

Product Creation:

Product creation is probably the easiest one to get really good at for most people. Not everyone of course will gravitate towards this one, but for most out there, it's the easiest one.

Anyone can get good at creating information products. It just takes focus. Even if you are not good at writing, you can pay someone to do the writing for you. Or, you can shoot videos... or audios.

But, researching and getting the valuable information and then packaging the information together into a valuable product is a skill that can easily be learned by anyone serious enough.

And, if you just got very good at just this... product creation... you can use that asset to make six figures. You could take your product and shop it around to people who control customers and can bring a lot of traffic.

You would be the one who created the very valuable product, and someone else would be the one who drives all the traffic.

At first glance you might be thinking... why would the person with traffic agree to do this? Well, this is a big insight for your to learn then... and here it is:

Marketers cannot create valuable products fast enough to meet the buying demands of their customers!

Read that a few times. It's true. And if you play your cards right, you can take that product you created and use it properly to land a solid Joint Venture with someone who has a big list.

That person would put their name on the product too. You just did a bunch of work for that person, and you'll make 50%. This is piggy back riding on other people's assets.

It happens all the time. But, for it to work, you have to have something of huge value to bring to the table. This is where most fail. They do not focus and get good at one thing. They are only 10% good at everything, so nobody wants to partner with them, barter and they have no assets.

Get really good at one thing, and create assets. If you are good at product creation, and anyone can get good at it, then you have an asset now. You can now use that asset as leverage.

When you have leverage, you can use that leverage as a tool to generate cash flow. Business is only a game of assets. You need to acquire assets to play the game.

If I own a building, I own an asset. I can slice the building up into offices and rent them out. I can have a social gathering at my building once a month to network with other business owners. I can rent out an office at a cheap price to an attorney or trade the office space for legal representation. I could do a lot. I can fix it up and sell it, take the extra cash and buy a car wash.

In this business, your assets will dictate your success and cash flow. If you can bring a ton of paid traffic, that's an asset. You are valuable and you can use that asset to get more assets.

Maybe someone comes to you, or you shop around your asset of massive traffic, and someone gives you half of their business for just driving the traffic.

Most people are not good at copywriting and it takes a lot of work to get good at it. If you are good at it, you have a massive asset. You can use that asset to earn more money and gain more assets.

Advanced level marketers usually have some assets. They usually have a nice list... can get traffic... have a name in the industry and key contacts... have some nice content or products that are valuable in the marketplace... can get joint venture affiliates... can create killer products... have the technical support or staff to handle things... and so on.

Intermediate level marketers never get there because they are holding themselves back and not getting really-really good at one specific thing. They are fearful and lack bold action taking abilities. They are lacking in the focus area and it's all a matter of just bringing it all together.

Intermediate level marketers can become advanced level marketers with focus, courage and mindset.

Assets + Assets = More Assets!

No assets = no income... just a dream.

If You Do Not Have The Money To Invest... Or The Skills Required... You Should Be Willing To Put In Time And Effort!

Remember when we talked about how little time there is for most people? Well, most people don't have time... don't have money... and don't have the knowledge required to make a bunch of money.

The good news is these are all excuses.

If you don't have time, then you are not serious enough and this is just a side hobby. Sleep less, watch less TV, rearrange your priorities and get time-wasting activities either eliminated or covered for you.

If you don't have money, then you have "time and effort" on your side. It's got to be time and effort because money does not magically show up. First, you do something and then money comes.

Many think like employees though. They think they have to get paid first then they'll work. This is a lazy mindset. Give me a job, pay me well, then I'll work hard. (wrong)

It does not work like that in business. You either come with an asset or you don't play the game. Your asset could be product creation or technical services.

I remember one guy coming to me and asking if he could partner with me. I asked him what his strengths were and he said technical. He was a software engineer and PHP programmer. He went on and on about his strengths as a software guy. But, at the end of the email he said... *"But I don't want to do that anymore and that's why I'm coming to you. I want to create a passive income".*

His one asset he had with me was his software creation abilities, but that's the one thing he would not do. And, to think, that's one of the big weakness I have, technical.

Opportunity lost.

What he should do instead is start where he is right now. His strength is technical, so use it as an asset to get more assets.

The Six Figure Equation!

Product + Traffic + Conversions = Six Figures!

When looking at the above equation, the question to ask is how good?

How good is your product?
How good is your traffic?
How good are your conversions?

Some people think (on the intermediate or lower levels) that all they have to do is toss up some product and money will come. NOT

Some people think all they have to do is write a few articles and money will come. NOT

Some people think they can write their own sales-copy even though they are not professional copywriters. NOT

It's not that it gets done, it's how good is it?

Let's compare Advanced level marketers with Intermediate level marketers (or newbies).

Here's what intermediate level marketers do:

They create their product by buying a PLR and writing a 10 page report to go with the PLR. They throw in some bonuses such as some other resell rights software product they have sitting on their desk top. Presto! They have a product.

It's not very good, but at least they have a product.

Next, they need copywriting, and copywriters are expensive, so they write it themselves. Bad move. No wonder it does not convert. (BTW, some do this for years and wonder where the money is hiding).

Next, they don't even drive traffic to it because by this time, they are already looking at some other product idea or opportunity. But, if they somehow do send traffic to it, it's a trickle and not very targeted. They never ask more than 4 people to promote it as affiliates either.

That's how it sort of goes.

Here's what advanced level marketers do:

They start with the idea and craft out the angles to sell the product. They first look at the market and the customers out there and they get in their heads and they figure out what the problems are... what's hot... what's not hot... what the customers hate, love, buy and are gravitating towards.

They analyze the potential customers. Sometimes they survey them and flat ask them what they want. They craft the sales message first. They hire a copywriter or they lay out a sales video and they focus on the sales pitch.

They map out the launch sequence and the sales process (upsells and downsells and backend). They set up an affiliate program and they write up a JV page to get people to sign up as affiliates.

They set up a JV blog... they make phone calls to people they don't know and they recruit them to promote the launch. They send emails and submit help tickets to other marketers (or people in their niche) to sign up as affiliates.

They set up tracking.

They focus hard on the sales pitch. They split test headlines. They get all the sales stuff in place, and then they make sure everything is working and the payment processing is working.

They then create killer content (or they just create content, maybe not killer content). Yep, many create the content last and a lot of people never create the content until after the product is even sold!

Like through webinars... maybe they are selling a six week webinar plan.

Here's the difference in a nutshell:

Advanced Marketers:

- **MORE traffic (A LOT MORE)**
- **More conversions (much better)**
- **Good technology**
- **Killer Product Creation**

PLUS:

- Long-term thinking and working on one launch for a long time (not just over a weekend and tossing something up there to see if it works).

Here's a measurement that should alert you to what you need to be doing. Below, on the graph, here's the MAJOR difference between newbies and Advanced marketers:

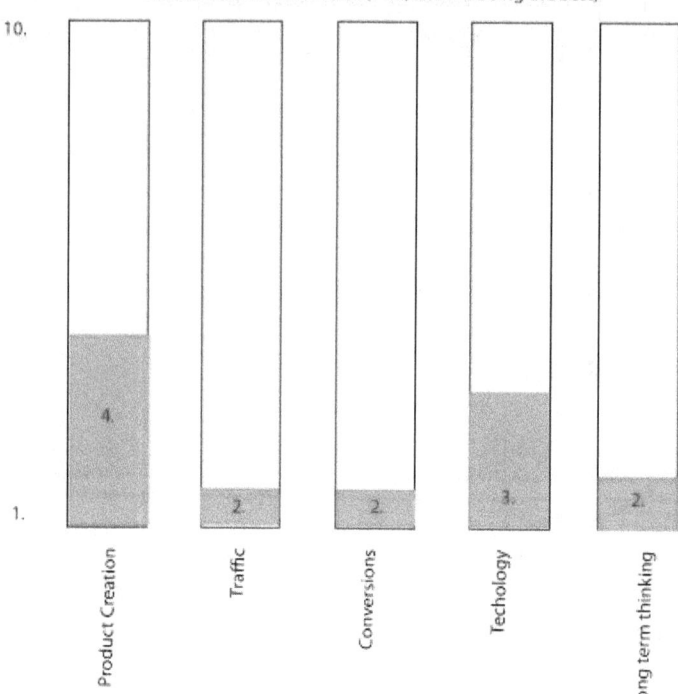

Newbie/Intermediate Level (1-10, with 10 being the best)

From looking above, you see a scale of 1 to 10, with 10 being the highest. Newbies/Intermediate rank sort of like the above. Yes, of course, not everyone is the same and some rank higher in certain areas, but this is a graph to follow yourself.

Rank yourself on the graph above.

How are you on traffic? Are you a 2? Or are you a 6? Maybe you are an 8? Maybe you are a 1.

How are you on conversions?
Here's the advanced graph:

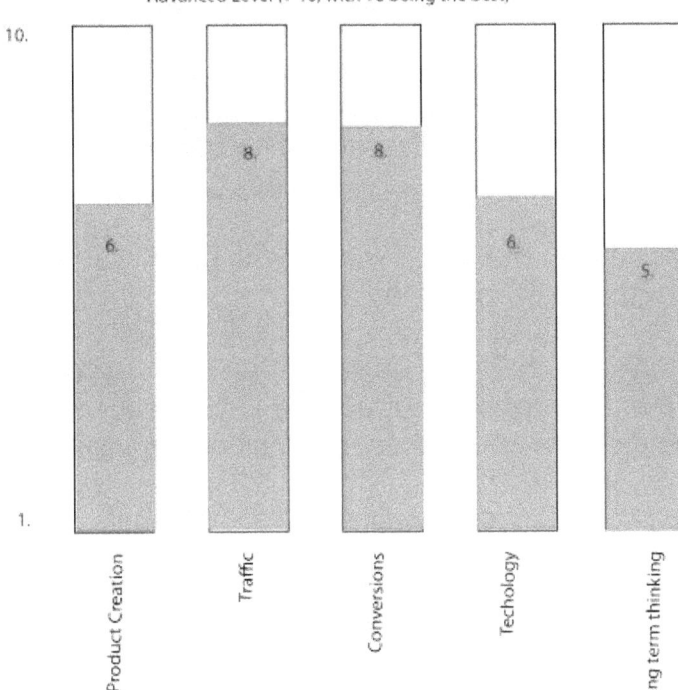

Advanced Level (1-10, with 10 being the best)

	Product Creation	Traffic	Conversions	Techology	Long term thinking
Score	6.	8.	8.	6.	5.

Notice how traffic and conversions are the highest? That's because that's where the money is made. Advanced level marketers only get a 6 on product creation and that's generous. Why? Because they understand the real money is in traffic and conversions that's why.

That's why a lot of advanced marketers get a bad name too sometimes, because they realize they don't have to have the greatest products ever created, they just need to be good enough.

Ouch?

Up to you to judge...

But what are the differences?

It's simple.

HOW GOOD are you at traffic? It's not that you cant drive traffic, because anyone can. Anyone can fire up Google Adwords or put $50 in Facebook advertising. Anyone can write up a few articles. Anyone can do that sort of stuff.

But, how good are you at traffic? The better you are, the more you'll make. The same goes for the other categories too.

For example, when you look at technology, it's easy to set up a paypal button. Anyone can do that... but what about upsells? What about down-sells? What about backend offers? What about continuity programs?

Basically, technology can equal more conversions. It can also equal more traffic and income. Do you use tracking? Do you split test headlines... or price points... or split test offers?

This should be a major breakthrough for you. You may not realize it, but right now, if you've read this and thought about what is being said here, you now realize where you are and where you need to get to, in order to make more money!

Its obvious then... when you look at the information provided so far... it's obvious to see why so many newbies are looking for magic buttons and pies in the sky. They want the easy way. Who doesn't?

And, because they are looking for the easy way, the magic button, they refrain from REALLY getting into what they are doing. They get a D- on their report card rather than an A-

Some get an F

Six Figure Equation:
Product + Traffic + Conversions = Six Figures!

When looking at the above equation, the question to ask is how good?

How good is your product?
How good is your traffic?
How good are your conversions?

I think a better way to look at this is this:

- Are you hasty?
- Are you looking for a quick fix?
- Do you jump around from a lot of different things?
- Do you forget what you were working on at times, only to say, "Oh yeah, that's what I was doing"?
- Do you catch yourself saying things like "I just need some quick income"?
- Do you rush to buy an IM product in hopes it's the answer you've been long looking for (sort of like rolling the dice)?
- How long do you spend focused on product creation?
- Do you find yourself getting tired of focusing on one thing and feel the need to stop working on one thing in order to work on something else?
- Do you find yourself logging off the computer after spending hours on it, only to find you got nothing done and was "reacting" the entire time?
- Do you find yourself multi-tasking a lot?
- When something is loading on your computer or you're saving something, do you rush to check your email real fast?
- When you turn on your computer, do you go to your email account first? (before getting any work done)?
- Do you catch yourself wondering what to work on when you get online... where you're looking for something to do?

Above in those graphs I showed you, one of the categories was "long term thinking". This is a dying concept because of the speed of the net and technology. Heck, I can stop writing this and check my Iphone and see who emailed me on three different email accounts in a matter of seconds.

Speed!

Society is getting faster and faster.

Our attention spans are getting shorter and shorter. It's no wonder so many kids have bad attention spans now and concentration problems... the television images move so fast on the TV and smart phones, and Ipads, and lap tops, and navigation systems and DVD TV's in the SUV's and multi-tabbed browsers and Skype and Facebook and Twitter and on and on.

Our ability to laser focus right now is a premium.

How good are you at product creation or traffic again?

It's no wonder so many people struggle to finish anything! Concentration levels are at a minimum. It's also due to the following...

It Does Not Cost Much At All To Start An Online Business And That Is Also <u>A HUGE PROBLEM</u>!

I can start a blog for nothing.

I can sell affiliate products and don't have to create anything myself.

I can slap Adsense ads on a page and earn money on clicks!

I can run special offers on popular marketing forums.

I can have a site up with nice graphics, hosting, an auto-responder and more for less than $100.

That means anyone can enter this business and that's a great thing. However it's also a bad thing too. It's bad because so many people fail because of it. They fail to finish things or have the business knowledge necessary to treat this like a business.

Basically, people start-up one thing on Monday... only to start up something completely different on Friday! They just don't treat this like a business.

Start treating this business as if you invested your life savings in it and that it depends on you, that you have burned the escape routes down and you now have no choice but to make it work.

Six figures is found on the other side of your ability to laser focus on one thing until it hurts so bad you can't stand it!

Six figures is waiting for you to get really good at:

- Product creation
- Traffic
- Conversions
- Tech
- Long term thinking
- Laser Focus
- Self Belief

The minute you realize this is the case... the minute you realize you have to get good at the above to make any kind of long term income... the minute you start taking action and improving these areas... that's the minute you start down the path to six figures. Your ability to stay on that path will get you there faster than you ever thought possible before.

The Best DAMN Step-By-Step Blueprint You Are Ever Going To Find!

Also By Eric Louviere

This is the quickest way to six figures I know.

Earning six figures online is going to come down to two main things:

TRAFFIC
And
CONVERSIONS

I preach this until it sinks in, but if you want to make a bunch of money, you're going to need to learn how to drive traffic and convert traffic!

If you are not making money online, it's because you are not driving traffic and converting that traffic.

What I'm about to cover in this report is exactly that. I'm going to give you point-blank insights for converting and for driving traffic and ultimately for making money and getting wealthy.

When you look to put the pieces together and finally start making money, then this report will take you through this step by step.

Now, I'm not going to write the salesletter for you, or install a squeeze page on your hosting provider, or make your up-sells work, or create products for you, but I'm certainly going to lay out a blueprint to follow step by step.

Get it all covered. Simply fill in the blanks and get each piece of the pie taken care of. I'm about to write a lot on conversions, because that's where the big money is found. Marketing is conversions. You need traffic, but you need to convert that traffic.

Most people either cannot convert or cannot drive traffic. I'll help you cover both in this step-by-step report. It's detailed, but you're also going to have to take the initiative and fill in any blanks you are missing.

For example, if you cannot get a squeeze page up and functional, you're going to need to pay attention to the part on "outsourcing". Let's get started.

Step One

Trade time for money, or build a real business that can generate passive income, or both.

Find an opportunity gap you can fill. In other words, find an opportunity... a need... a want... in your marketplace, and fill it! This is going to require you to look at yourself in the mirror and ask yourself...

"What am I good at already?"

If you do this and find you are not good at anything yet, then this is the question to answer:

"What CAN I get good at fast?"

What I'd recommend you do is figure out what you gravitate towards. Are you interested in copywriting and conversions... traffic... technology... product creation... contacts... teaching... designing... managing people... researching... what?

You are going to need to pick one and get good at something. It's called specialized knowledge and it could be the quickest way to six figures from home there is.

For example, people need traffic. Right now, back-links and social marketing and SEO is hot. It's hot and people are buying those kinds of services.

I could provide:

- Manual submission to online directories
- Press releases to 50 different press release directories
- Social bookmarking to 50 different sites like Digg, etc
- Articles written and submitted

And so on...

That's a valuable service right now. People all over the place are buying similar services.

There are other types of services to provide too. Tons of them. Think of all the things people want and need. How can you supply them?

But wait...

This is work Eric!

This is hard!

This requires Time!

Aren't there a lot of services like this already?

How can I do this in an affordable manner and still be competitive and still make profits?

Welcome to the beautiful, rewarding, challenging and marvelous world of "business". Isn't it spectacular?

All excuses and challenges and obstacles are but only a creative idea away from being banished and out of your mind! There's opportunity everywhere because most people have those exact same excuses.

The only difference between six figure earners and non-six-figure earners are the six figure earners ignored those excuses and did it anyway! They found a way to make it work! They picked a target and went for it.

You have to start where you are and have faith you can accomplish your goals. You have to have faith that if any obstacle arises, you will find a way around it, over it, to the side of it or right through it.

[Step One]

Find an opportunity gap and fill it. Create a real business, a service and provide people with what they need and want. Research and figure out what people want and provide it.

I know a marketer who made millions online. He sold his empire and started a "web design" business. He had a huge massive list of people, tons of products, all kinds of contacts, and he sold it all, only to start up a service.

I asked him why. He said, "There's more money in web design across the world and I think I'm a good enough marketer to get a huge slice of that pie".

The reason so many online marketers started earning a bunch of money in the "offline small business" market is because they started thinking like this. They started ignoring the "pie's in the sky" and started creating real businesses and services.

Start researching what the market needs and provide a service!

Step 2

Create a real online business that can generate passive daily income for you! It's going to require something you've heard before...

This passive income is going to require you dig down and finally get serious about building a list. It's that simple. Almost every single marketer I know who earns six figures or more has a list of subscribers.

And, some don't even have that big of a list, and still earn six figures from that list. It's one of the easiest ways to six figures I've ever seen!

But, that list must be responsive.

And, that's the problem for most people. Well, strike that. That's the second biggest problem for most marketers. The biggest one is how to start that list.

2 Challenges:

1. Where and how do you start a list from scratch?
2. How do you make that list responsive?

First off, there's a thousand different ways to do this. But, let's keep it clear, you need traffic and you need conversions to build a list.

Then, you need to "warm that list up" to YOU.

You have to "turn them on" to YOU.

More on that in a second.

Step 3

You need to create something valuable to give away free to get subscribers. You need a squeeze page or a system for capturing subscribers.

- You need a place to drive traffic to.
- That place must capture subscribers.

What will you give away free?

- An ebook/report
- An e-course
- A newsletter
- Videos
- Audios
- Etc

First, you must find something valuable that people WANT and that thing you are giving away must be presented in the RIGHT way to get subscribers to opt in.

This is where conversions come in.

But, first, how do you get something valuable to give away free?

You either **A)** create it yourself or **B)** buy it

For example, you could interview some advanced marketers and give away the transcripts and up-sell the audios. Or, if it's just written, you can give away the transcript/report of the interview.

But again, it's the conversions which are important. That's the key most miss. It's not good enough to just go grab or just go create something to give away free, it needs to convert!

Step 4

How do you convert?

Well, first ask yourself the question, what would make you opt in? I mean, you are sort of your market and to think about what would cause you to opt in is a good start.

Curiosity works to a point. Value works. Fancy looking graphics can work to a point. Let's break it down.

People opt in because they *want something*.

Today, people don't opt in as easily as they used to. People are getting tired of spam and emails pounding the daylights out of their inbox. So, you have to stand out above the noise.

But, you just need to give them what they want!

What does the market want?

In the IM space here's what they want:

- **Freedom**
- **A blueprint system that works**
- **Proof**
- **Simplicity**
- **Time savers**
- **They want to be less frustrated**
- **They want to make income fast**
- **They want tools**
- **They want a list**

- **They want traffic**
- **They want to be successful**
- **They want gossip and entertainment**

Most squeeze pages are boring... "Opt in here to get my 7 steps to Internet Riches!"

Yeah right.

Imagine a video on a squeeze page that says...

"I was sick and tired of being sick and tired so I paid a high priced mentor to teach me about driving traffic. He schooled me for 2 hours on nothing but TRAFFIC! This guy does about $400,000 online too! He just let it rip. I was allowed to record the entire call. Aside from a few curse words, this recording is incredible. He lays out exactly how he uses PPC and how he uses ClickBank.com to get affiliates. He has a genius way of building that traffic into a list. I recorded the entire thing! As a special marketing test, I'm giving it to you for FREE today! But, you're going to have to hurry because I'm thinking of selling this recording for big bucks."

There's a reason why: "Special marketing test I'm running"

There's urgency: "I'm thinking of selling this"

There's curiosity... value... it has desire... it has credibility... it has a lot of copywriting factors just in that one paragraph.

But you know what; nobody knows how it will do until you send it traffic. Then, you have a measurement of how many clicks came and how many opted in. You'll have an opt-in rate. And, from there, you can tweak.

You see, most squeeze pages you find out there do not have a "reason why" they are giving something away free. You see that on salesletters (reason why) but you don't see that on squeeze pages often.

You need a "reason why" you are giving something away free.

This is a huge insight for squeeze pages most people will never realize. Your "reason why" can boost your opt-in conversions.

Here's how it goes:

- Pick your niche market
- Create or buy something valuable to give away free in exchange for subscribers. (true value)
- Create a squeeze page that is compelling, that uses copywriting psychology to convert. If need-be, hire a copywriter.
- Provide the visitors with a "reason why" you are giving that value away free. Have a reason, or they'll think it's crap and that's why it's free.
- Hit on curiosity factors, make them opt-in to get "the rest of the story"

You need to focus on conversions here and this is where most people fail. They may not be good at conversions themselves yet. Copywriters who are familiar with the marketplace often have a knack for what will convert. Advanced marketers have this "knack" too. Many newbies do not have their pulse on the emotions of the marketplace yet. Therefore, they often misfire when it comes to crafting a compelling squeeze page or opt-in formula.

Step 5

Ever heard of a two-step approach?

This is popular in direct mail. In fact, here's the truth... if you want to know what works, it's the fundamentals of direct response marketing. That's it. Forget the magic and sizzle in the sky, to make a ton of money, you need the fundamentals of direct response marketing.

Without those insights and fundamentals, you're just chasing a scheme... and schemes rarely work or last. It's chasing a buck and it's temporary. What works is:

Product + Traffic + Conversions = Sales!

Ok, back on track here. Let's talk about a huge insight – the two step approach!

Let us assume that most of the world has caught on now, and they are resistant to entering their names and emails to get stuff free, because they now know they will get a bunch of pitching emails that are trying to sell them stuff.

Even my wife, who is not into IM hates opting into stuff now.

Therefore, coming with a unique approach can be powerful. This is how it works.

Instead of having one single landing page where they have to enter their name and email address to continue, come with two pages instead.

On the first page, have them answer a few questions (multiple choice) and then click a "continue" button to move to the next page. This will get the visitors "engaged" in the process more and they could be more likely to opt in on the second page.

For example, your fist page might have a headline, some copy (content) and then 4 questions on it.

- How much weight would you like to lose in the next 60 days?

- How often do you exercise each week?

- Do you drink sodas?

- How many hours of sleep per day do you get?

Then, there would be a continue button.

On the next page, at the top, could be a short screen cam video that gives them 3 tips to losing weight. At the end of that video, you could pitch them on opting in to get your "Top 10 Insights For Losing 30 Pounds Or More Very Easily! 100% Free as a special marketing test! Limited and is likely to close soon"

At this point, they are engaged into the process and the content. They did not just do a quick drive-by of your site. They answered some questions and then watched a short video. They are warmed up a bit and are engaged. They are pre-framed on your content (because they watched your teaser video).

They got a taste of your personality (if you shot the video) and they are more likely to buy something or follow you now. Who do we buy from? We buy from those we know, like and trust.

This two step approach can be a fantastic way to increase conversions. Plus, for some paid traffic sources out there, it does not get slapped as often.

Make that site look nice and attractive with professional graphics, and you could be sitting on a winner!

Step 6

At this point, you know you need a squeeze page that gives something away free (something valuable)... and you have some clear insights on how to convert better on that squeeze page.

Your aim right now is to build a list and *to warm that list up to you*, so it becomes responsive. This is conversions too!

Most marketers like to hit-people-over-the-heads with sales attempts and sell the snot out of them hardcore. If you think about that for a second, do you like to be sold hardcore? Probably not

Therefore, it's critical to understand that you need to be well prepared to eliminate that skepticism they have as much as possible. It's paramount that you get visitors to trust you more. You want to tip the scale of "trust" over to your side.

Assume that everyone is deeply skeptical. They are. They are not going to A) opt in easily or B) buy something easily. People are becoming harder and harder to sell online (or offline) because money is tight and they think twice before buying stuff more than ever.

Plus, competition is expanding and there are more and more people competing for the same dollars you are trying to get. What you should know is the magical insight to conversions!

It's called:

PROOF!

Proof factors are the factors on which you should sell. You should always look to do your marketing and selling based on proof factors! You could convert tons more people than your competition if you focus on proof!

Proof and social proof trump almost everything else when it comes to conversions. And, let me be the one to tell you this:

To be a great marketer is to be a great converter!

Traffic is easy. Anyone can drive traffic in the next 20 minutes by running a PPC campaign. Traffic is easy. Conversions are hard. The money is found in conversions.

It starts with the first impression of you and lasts all the way through to where they are paying you thousands of dollars for consulting. From a free subscriber to a VIP client, proof factors and conversions and warming them up to you is where the conversions are found.

How do you get proof factors?

You do this through making your subscribers and customers raving fans of yours. You do this on purpose and you set it up ahead of time.

For example, I could email my lists right now and tell them I have a product I'd like them to review. I am only going to allow 10 people to get this product for free, because I want feedback and testimonials.

I follow up with them and stay on them (because people are not easy to get testimonials from) about getting me feedback. I know most will love it, but getting them to say it is another story.

One method is to incentivize them. Here's an example I've used before... I might do a 4 week webinar course and then give the customers a bonus of two more weeks. However, to gain access to weeks 5 and 6, they need to fill out a survey form. That survey form is geared to get me testimonials.

Proof factors and social proof play a huge role in conversions now-a-days. Think about all the review sites online. Think about the transparency we now see on the net. Everything is out in the open now. Word gets around fast. People review and post those reviews everywhere. Use this to your advantage by turning your customers into raving fans of yours.

It is not good to simply toss up some piece of crap product and sell it. People talk. Customers will quickly post their frustrations with you. That can kill a business fast.

However, if you get raving fans... social proof sells like hot cakes. Case studies, endorsements, testimonials (be careful with income claims), review sites, buzz, over-delivering, unannounced bonuses, etc

Step 7

Further warming up your list...

Look, this is critical. There are tons of lists and your subscribers are not just on YOUR list. They are all over the place... likely on multiple lists... and are getting hit with advertising messages from every direction.

Think about it for a second... how many lists are you on? And, how many email accounts do you have? Are you on Facebook and Twitter... Linked In, etc?

Do you visit forums? You are likely getting hit from all directions too. There's a ton of noise out there and that noise is getting louder and louder.

To rise above the noise, you have to be different.

You have to capture your subscribers' attention and turn them on to YOU. Get them engaged in you and your material. You can do this many ways, but the core concept is what's important.

Warm them up to you. Turn them on to you. Brand yourself to your list. Use your own name a lot in emails to them, on blogs, on pages... etc.

If you look at my site, my name jumps out at you and so does that wicked looking picture of me:

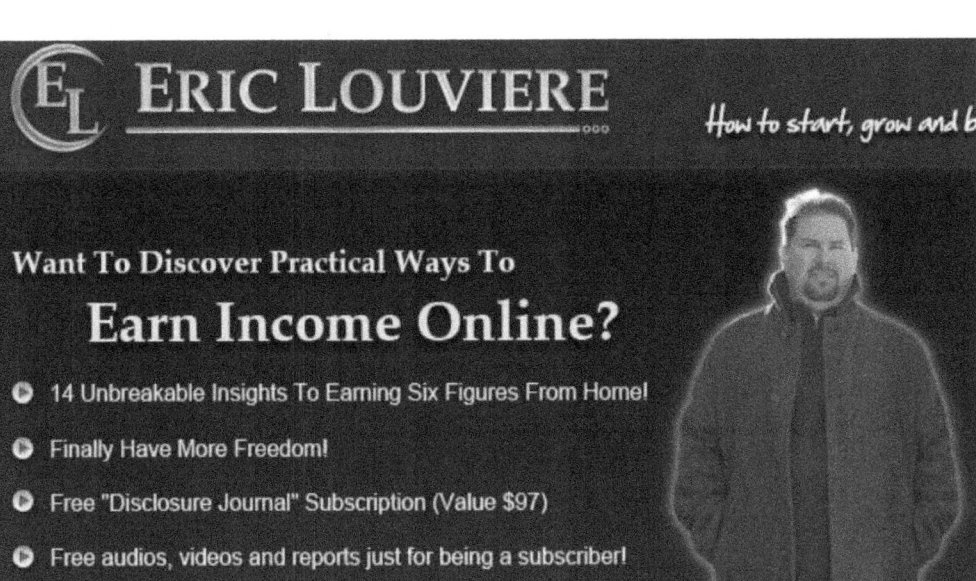

Positioning

Look, I don't really care about what the "herd" says about gurus... all the guru bashing... it's irrelevant and it's a given in our society. Criticism is a given and is expected no matter what. You should expect criticism if you are doing "above average" things.

If you are NOT average, then that means you're investing in yourself. You are investing in your dreams. You are taking the types of actions, most people NEVER take!

Average people don't read books like this. Average people watch TV and play video games and spend their time on trivial things.
Average people don't even mess with "businesses" or even think about quitting jobs to work from home. Now, they might "think" about it or wish for it, but they certainly don't take action!

So, expect criticism.

And with that in mind, you need to abide by the number one law of publicity:

Toot... Toot... Toot your own horn.

Because nobody is going to toot your horn until you toot your own horn. Nobody is going to treat you like an expert, until you act like an expert, talk like an expert and think like an expert.

People buy from those they KNOW, LIKE and TRUST! They trust experts. (see doctors, attorneys, celebrities, authors, speakers, product owners, etc)

I have a buddy who contacted a guy who owns his own site and publishes a newsletter and free videos. He was excited when that guy responded to him. He's an expert!

Later, he found out he's not that successful. However, he certainly appeared that way to my friend. Why? Because he did videos and audios and had his own product with his picture on the page and spoke to an audience.

That is NOT viewed at as "average".

Therefore, that guy on that site with the audios and YouTube videos was an expert! Sure, he knew what he was talking about on those videos, but so did my friend! In fact, my friend might know more than he does on the subject!

If I studied "How To Write Press Releases" for a couple months, I'd know more about that than 95% of the entire population, including most of the people who write press releases!

Ok, now... let's get to the main point of warming people up. YOU HAVE TO DO IT! There's too much noise out there. Rise above the noise. Here's how to do it:

- Be, act, think, speak, walk and write like and expert (like an authority).
- Be a leader (herd follows)
- Be entertaining (herd is bored)
- Be yourself (herd like's real people)
- Be controversial at times (herd likes gossip)
- Give quality free stuff (herd likes free)
- Put yourself out there (herd needs to see you and hear you and know you)
- Be different (herd is bored)
- Embellish some of your personality characteristics (herd is bored and busy and you need to stand out)
- Associate yourself with other experts/celebrities in the niche (law of association and herd automatically pegs you as an expert too!)
- Joint Venture with other experts (herd likes variety)
- Tap into their emotions (herd is an emotional people)

Let's say you are brand new and are just starting up your list. Let's say you are in the Real Estate Investing niche. You are going to sell, market and provide information to people who want to make big bucks in the REI market.

So, you set up a squeeze page like instructed and you give away something valuable free to capture subscribers. You then hit them with sales attempts. You email them and sell them affiliate offers or your own product offers.

Then, you notice that most of them don't buy. Hmm... what could be wrong? Maybe it's the salesletter? Maybe they don't want to buy that product?

So, you decide to give it away free. You hate giving it away free, but since nobody bought it, why not? You know it's good quality but it's not selling... so you give it away free to your list.

The next thing you know, people are emailing you about how awesome it is... they are asking you questions... asking you if you have a course they can buy... asking you if you do mentoring... etc.

The next time you sell something, it should sell much better.

I write a journal called "Disclosure Journal". They are reports I write and give to my subscribers free from time to time. Those reports are better than many paid reports out on the market (not my words or my opinion, but the opinion of the readers of that report). No joke.

Well, in that report, I subtly mention that I do 1-on-1 mentoring. I've received more mentoring clients from those reports than just about anything I've ever done.

It's because they read the report and see how incredible the content is. They learn stuff and they get "ah ha" moments and get motivated to succeed.

And

They

Get

Turned

On

To

Me!

One marketer I know, years ago, provided a free e-course to subscribers. It was on SEO techniques. I was one of his subscribers and I was absolutely glued to his emails. I devoured his free material.

Later, he launched a software program and it sold like hot cakes. The IM market snatched it up and it was one of the top products of the year. He turned everyone on to him and warmed them up to him and turned himself into a raging success very quickly.

Information Marketer

That means you market information. You distribute information. You relay information. Think about that for a second.

We operate on the Internet (The Information Super Highway!). We are marketers who distribute information to those who WANT that information (niche).

Where is information found? Everywhere! It's free all over the place too! So, why sell it? You sell it because people buy it, that's why. You find a place where people are buying all sorts of stuff and you just get in the way of all that money being spent.

I once gathered a ton of free articles online about a specific topic. I copied them, pasted them into a PDF and sold the report for $5!

People thanked me for providing them with all those links, and resources and for doing the hard "research" work for them.

As an information marketer, you should know that you have access to tons of information. It's all over the place. You can simply research a topic, master it, and sell it!

Just make sure it's a topic where tons of people are already buying. Sell what they are already buying. Sell what they are buying right now. Find out what people are buying... and go sell that to them.

Step 8
CONVERSIONS!

Now that you understand how powerful "positioning" is and why you should warm up and turn on your subscribers to you... let's talk more about conversions...

First of all, conversions = marketing.

If you are not converting, you are not making money. This entire book could be ONLY about conversions and you would be a smart camper to have read this far.

There's nothing more important than "conversions" when it comes to marketing. You might think it's traffic... and certainly traffic is critical... but traffic is not the key to success in online marketing.

Its conversions...

Sure, traffic is sexier and sells better and more people are interested in traffic than conversions. And, most people think traffic is the key to success online, but it's not.

Its conversions...

You might be able to get 100,000 visitors to a blog, but if that blog is not converting into dollars, it's almost use-less. You might have Adsense links all over that blog and affiliate banners, but if nobody clicks them, you make zero.

It is conversions...

The Highest Forms Of Conversions:

1. Celebrity/Star Power
2. Expert/Authority
3. Salesmanship
4. Useful

The highest form of conversions is "Star Power". There's a reason why celebrities earn so much money. The herd loves them some star power!

Tiger Woods plays golf, but he earns millions from endorsements. A guru in the IM space who is considered a celebrity in our market, can sell a product for $2,500 on list building and get tons of sales... where most others in the market can't... even if their product is superior to the gurus' list building product.

Now, not all of us want to be some celebrity. However, that does not take away from the fact; celebrity is the highest form of conversions.

Next on the list is "Expert/Authority" level. If you are in legal trouble, are you going to listen to a friend at the bar give you advice... or pay an attorney thousands of dollars?

If you need heart surgery, are you going to trust some nurse on what to do? No, you'll go to a heart surgeon. Specialize knowledge is extremely powerful – and lucrative!

Next on the list is "Salesmanship". That's where copywriting and slick persuasion techniques come in. Sure, this can be used on all levels to convert and this is what most people think of when it comes to conversions. They think, "Sales copy".

And, this can convert well too!

This is where you see nobody's come out of nowhere fast, and make a huge splash of sales with their product. The sales copy converted like crazy!

A marketer can have a crappy product, but if the sales copy is great, it'll sell like hot cakes. Now, it might have a huge refund percentage, but it'll sell great!

Last on the list is "usefulness".

This is a product that's extremely useful to lots of people. It does not need to be great... or even have sales copy. It can convert because it's very useful and helps people.

I tend to think of software or scripts that are very use-full and are tools to save time, energy and money.

Step 9
"Conversions... Conversions... Conversions!"

You are either a copywriter or you are not. If you are not, then you need help in that area in order to succeed online. If you are not a copywriter, then you need to do one of two things:

- Learn it and get good at it yourself
- Pay someone or partner with someone who is strong at it

That's it. If you are not good at copywriting, then copywriting could be a huge road block that's preventing you from moving forward in your business.

Seriously, are you good at copywriting? If not, you need to get it covered. Yes, I'm talking about sales videos too. Some people are terrible at sales videos and copywriting and they continue to try and sell their own stuff and wonder where the sales are hiding?

But, it's not all about copywriting and sales videos either. It's about branding and turning people on to you. It's about warming up people to you. It's about building anticipation. There's a lot that goes into making sales.

Testimonials are a big deal as well for conversions.

The conversion Cheat Sheet!

There are some main components to a salesletter (or sales video) and you need to nail all of them. Here are the components:

1. Headline

You need a compelling headline. This headline is designed to do one major thing and that's "capture attention". People are busy, bored, multi-tasking and then land on your sales message.

Your job with the headline is to capture them, disrupt their flow and get them engaged into your copy. This can also be called a "pattern interrupt".

Basically, with a pattern interrupt, you grab their attention by doing something that makes them take notice. You could say something off the wall, something bold and controversial. Here's an example:

All The Gurus Are Lying To YOU!

See how that shakes them up a bit at first glance of your page? This can also be applied to sales videos too. When they first start watching your video, you should "capture their attention" and disrupt their flow!

A headline can be benefit driven as well. Think of what your big benefit is... your big money phrase. Find out what is the main reason people will buy this product. Then, craft a headline that uses that benefit.

This is also where you find a "hook" or a big promise to offer people. You could be a good "hook" away from having a high converting sales letter. It's that big of a deal.

For example, I had a program where the headline was something like this:

Get A Membership Site In 15 Minutes!

Basically, the headline says it all. In a matter of seconds, they have the main point of the letter and the rest of the letter just supports the headline and turns them on even more!

Here are some of the headline formats I personally love to use:

If You Want To _____, Then This Program Will _____ For You!

This is basically an "If you, then..." headline.

Another way to start a headline is:

What If...

I also like using these on bullet points and sub-headlines throughout my copy. This is a big conversion technique right here. "What if" is simply a question and is painting a picture. You are not necessarily saying this is going to happen, but are implying this could happen.

What If you started getting thousands of clicks to your site this week?

What if you could convert at 5%?

What if you could launch a flurry of traffic to any site, any time you wanted to?

What if you earned a passive income that allowed you to quit your job and live a lazy lifestyle?

And so on...

Another technique is to simply start out your headline with the word "How"

How To Read This Report And Make Yourself A Bazillion Dollars!

Of course, the famous: "Who Else..." headlines always tend to be good ones...

Who else wants to earn money from home very easily with PPC?

Your headline is quite important. It's the first impression and you need to nail it.

With headlines, I like to use:

Impact font size 25 to 40
Tahoma font size 18 or 20
Georgia font size 16 to 20
Verdana font size 18 to 20
Arial font size 18 to 20

2. The sub headline

The sub headline is designed to hit them with more benefits and get them to continue reading the letter. Its purpose is to engage them further and support the headline, and pass them on to the rest of the letter.

One of my favorite sub headlines is:

For reasons you'll understand in just a moment, this letter will showcase why this report is the best report you've never read before!

That sub-headline hooks them, engages them to read further and pre-frames them that this is very valuable.

3. Your introduction

This is also very important. When you introduce yourself, you are still on a first impression basis and you're still trying to get them to read the letter. You want to engage them and get them to make a mental decision to read your letter.

You will introduce yourself here, but you will need to also capture them further. You can do this with a powerful story. Your story can follow this format:

1. Here's what I used to do
2. That did not work
3. I was frustrated, wasted time, energy and money
4. I got obsessed to find the answers
5. Here's what I found
6. I tested it and it worked
7. I tested it again and it worked even better
8. I shared it with others and it worked for them too
9. Here's what most people usually do (I used to do that too)
10. That's why they all fail (like I used to fail)
11. Here's what works and you should do this too (or continue failing like everyone else)

4. Proof factors

We already discussed this earlier, but as part of the format, this is where you need to make sure you tap into proof factors (testimonials, case studies, endorsements, screen shots, video proof, audio proof, social proof, comments, publicity, etc etc). Pepper your sales letter with all of the above if you can.

5. Homer Simpson Level

Your prospects have to "get it". They have to understand exactly what it is and what they get when they buy. By Homer Simpson, I mean, even his dumb brain should get it.

Don't sell to your level; sell to the Homer Simpson level so everyone gets it. I'm not being rude, this is true. It's a big mistake tons of marketers make time and time again. They sell to their own level, instead of the mass market's level.

Describe your product – point blank – as to what it is and what they get when they buy it. Be direct and to the point as possible. Cover the features and benefits of the product.

6. Reason Why

You have to have a reason why you are selling this product. If it's so great, why are you selling it? If it's so cheap, why is it so cheap? If it's so valuable, why is it not more expensive?

Many marketers miss this too. Reason why: I am selling this because I used to be just like you and I always wished someone would provide something like this. But, you have to have skin in the game or you wont follow it. Therefore, it's not free.

I did all the hard work for you and did all the research for you, so because of that, I'm putting a nominal price on this.

7. Bullet Points

Bullet points can make the difference between conversions a lot of times. Bullet points need to be mini-headlines. They need to spark curiosity, but fuel benefits. They need to be emotional and tap into the emotions your market feels.

Make your bullet points stand out and command attention. Here are some formats of bullet points:

How to _____
How to make sure you always _____
When not to _____
3 tricks to _____
1 little secret, when missed causes _____ to happen
Why most people ___ when they should _____ instead
The 7 step formula for doing _____
The _____ technique

Another thing you can do to jazz up your bullet points is to add action words to make them even more powerful, adjectives and verbs, such as:

Tightly created cheat sheets designed to _____
Incredible steps to _____
Tremendous secret for forcing _____
Mind-numbing method for _____
Super dynamo way to _____

8. Overcome objections

This is critical. You must stop and think. You have to put yourself in the shoes of the customers and ask yourself, "why would I NOT buy?" What reasons would cause me to not buy?

If possible, get feedback from those who did not buy. Ask them point blank, why did you not buy? Give them a gift for answering the question. If possible, go ahead and give them free what they did not buy just to get the feedback. It's that valuable.

Figuring out why they did not buy, can help you overcome those objections and just watch your conversions fly! I could give you 100 examples of salesletters that failed because of one tiny objection that was not overcome in the salesletter, but was obvious to customers. Think like a customer.

You can spell out the objections right there on the page:

Why do I need to know about conversions Eric?

Because it's that important. You could be missing out on tons of money and failing miserably because you continue to ignore "conversions". Traffic is one thing, conversions is another. You need both! Most ignore conversions.

(See? I stated the objection above in red and overcame the objection)

9. Who does not need your product (who it's not for)

This is a classic technique where you list out all the people who this product is not for. For example:

- This is not for tire kickers
- It is not for pie in the sky seekers
- It is not for advanced gurus who know it all
- It is not for get rich quick seekers

You can tell them what the product is not:

- This is not MLM
- This is not PPC
- This is not a get rich quick scheme

You can tell them what they don't need to know:

- You don't need to know PPC
- You don't need contacts
- You don't need a list
- You don't need to be technical

10.   Stack the value!

At this point, you want to tell them what it is point blank again and stack the value. For example, you spent 4 years learning this and 40 hours per week doing it. You worked hard to learn all this and they get it instantly. This is worth years of experience.

You can stack the value on dollars too. For example, the software is worth $1,000 alone and I'm also giving you 1-on-1 mentoring, which I normally charge $500 for. Plus, I'm giving you my blueprint report, normally valued at $127.

This is where you can add in bonuses, of course.

11.   Price it.

You get all this value for the low price of only _____. Test your prices as well. Sometimes a higher price converts better than a lower price. Test it and see.

12.   Bold Guarantee!

Listen, the number one reason people don't buy from you is because they DON'T BELIEVE YOU. They just don't believe your claims. Therefore, if you give them a crazy, bold guarantee, your conversions can sky rocket.

Don't believe me? Try it out yourself. Offer a double your money back guarantee, or a 365 day guarantee and see what happens. Your conversions will sky rocket.

13. Closing Statement!

In sales, you have to close people to get the money. You have to ask for the sale. However, most salesletters you see never ask for the sale and they never close strong. They build up the value throughout the salesletter and then close with some wimpy statement.

Close strong!

Coffee is for closers! (That's from a movie)

Take your headline and turn it into a closing statement. Hit them between the eyes. Tell them they will either continue to have the problem they have, or they will solve it by buying your product!

Hit on the pain again. Agitate the pain. Close strong.

14. PS's

This is one of the most read portions of your salesletter. Make them strong and spend good quality time on them. You can restate the guarantee, hit them with a new benefit, hit them with the bonuses and hit them with the "money phrase" (i.e. get a membership in 15 minutes!)

15. Contact Us

Despite your best attempt to make a sale, people will still have questions. How would you like to make money just for answering simple email questions? Then, put your email or phone number or both at the bottom of the page. Most refrain from doing this and they miss out. Now, if you sell tons and tons of products, maybe you could just put your help desk link there and let your staff handle it, but if you're a one person show, take that and use it as a opportunity.

Sidebar advice:

I want to take this moment and give you a technique I've used many times that works great. It's a little bit more work, but it converts like crazy. Here it goes (thank me later):

When you have a list of subscribers, send them an email and ask them to email you back if they are interested. Then, email them the salesletter as a PDF. Interact with them via email too. Answer their questions.

You will be surprised at how many sales you make. I believe this works for many reasons. One is... nobody does this so it's different! Another reason is they believe you more when they interact with you via email.

I've done this with high ticket products and services and I've generated well over 100k with this method alone.

16.   Scarcity

Scarcity is huge. If you put a limit on your products, they will sell much better than if it's open forever. Some kind of scarcity can certainly increase conversions. You can hit them with a limited number of copies will ever be sold. You can hit them with a price scarcity (price goes up on Monday)... and so on.

You could put a limit on your products and sell only 100, and sell out fast. But, if you left it open forever, maybe it took you six months or more to sell 100 and convert well.

Instead, go for getting the highest conversions now! Create other products to sell later or come out with a 2.0 version later.

17.   Know your market!

This may seem obvious, but it's not. Knowing your market well (real well) can skyrocket your income fast. Do not discount this section off, as it has real power when you realize it's dynamics.

You see, if you know how your market thinks, what frustrates them, what they like, love, desire, gravitate towards, what their problems are, what they need, what's lacking in their business, what the biggest road blocks are or speed bumps that get in their way, what their beliefs are, etc then you can tap into that.

If you know your customers better than your competition does, then you can win and earn more money. I'm not saying there is a lack of abundance or a lack of dollars out there at all. I'm saying that when you know your market better than competitors, then you can be more creative and understand how to sell and provide for your market.

You want to satisfy your market's desires. Give them what they desire. Sell what they want, more than what they need or what you think they need. Don't sell them what you want them to have or what you think they need, sell them what they want!

In the IM market, they want:

- A magic button
- A business in a box
- Traffic
- Blueprint methods
- Schemes
- Black hat tricks
- A list
- Passive income
- Power
- Freedom
- Security
- To be popular
- To be special, famous, be someone

- To be able to buy things and impress others
- To be comfortable
- To be lazy and work less
- To be accepted and admired

They are extremely skeptical. Therefore, you must hit on all the elements mentioned above as best you can to counter that skepticism. You must give them a bold guarantee or risk reversal to counter that skepticism. The better you are at countering that skepticism, the more money you're going to make.

One of the reasons (there's many) why gurus convert so well, is there is not as much skepticism for buying their products. They are proven and public and there's tons of social proof out there for them. They have star appeal. Sure, it's not going to counter all skepticism, but a lot of it.

Your ability to minimize skepticism is the key to conversions.

18. Fears

Fear is one of the most incredible driving emotions. Fear propels people, it sabotages people, it limits people, and it cripples people from taking action or buying. Fear is a dominant emotion is most people.

I don't know how many times someone has emailed me or told me, "I can't buy this at this time because my wife would be very upset".

So, use it to your advantage in conversions.

What are your markets 3 to 5 biggest fears in buying your product... or using your product? How can you overcome those fears?

Next, what fears "in life" does your market have? In the IM market, many have fears of being homeless, losing money, failing, feelings of being inadequate or a lesser person. How can you tap into those fears and solve them for customers?

Peace of mind, security and protection is a real driving force. Many just want to relax and not be stressed out and they are willing to work hard, be workaholics, and chase their dreams forever just to find some kind of peace of mind from bills, money problems, stress, job demands, bosses, traffic and problems in general.

People connect money and financial freedom to happiness. That's a thought in their minds already and it's your job (if in this market) to tap into those thoughts, images in their heads and conversations already going on in their minds.

19.   Identity

This is one of my favorite topics. It's just fascinating and it's extremely powerful for making money, persuasion, influence and conversions!

Take note of the following emotional triggers:

Vanity: (fame, recognition, being popular, admired, respected, etc)

Peace of mind: (relaxation, relief, security, ease, easy, lazy, freedoms)

Self Improvement: (getting to the next level, higher achievement, advancement, better person, better body, healthier, more money, more spiritual, more happiness, better relationships, more life)

Greed: (control, pride, competition, revenge, power, etc)

Those above are powerful emotional triggers to tap into one's identity. Think about all the different ways you can tap into those identity areas in your copy and advertising.

These are all big in the IM space. With vanity, you can tap into how people want to be admired, respected and popular.

20.   What are people in your market currently HOT about?

One of the smartest insights you could learn is:

Figure out what everyone is buying, and go sell it to them!

But, I want you to think about that more. In the IM space, certain things get hot. I remember when Adsense was very hot and everyone was buying anything and everything about Adsense. It was an easy sell. If you wanted to make some quick and easy money, all you'd have to do is interview a few Adsense experts, wrap up the audios into a package and sell the heck out of it.

You can easily find out what's hot in your market right now... research, craft a product and an offer, and sell it. Anyone can. But, your ability to pay attention to your market can earn you a ton of money.

This is why I recommend to many of my VIP clients that they pick one market they are passionate about and stick to it. They will get to know that market better and better, and they'll constantly be looking for opportunity gaps. They will constantly be on the lookout for an opportunity to earn more money by delivering HOT information the market is crazy about right now!

21.   Why is buying your product a smart purchase?

What are all the reasons, your product is a smart purchase? For me, when writing copy, I try and think about the logical reasons why people would buy what I'm selling.

There are emotional reasons, and we certainly try to tap into those emotions in the "make money" space, but tapping into the logical reasons is also quite important too. Some people rationalize the purchase and dwell on the decision before buying. Others buy very quickly with impulse buys.

Therefore, if you spend some time thinking about all the reasons why it's a smart decision, this can pay off huge for you! Reasons such as: saves time, money, energy... will keep you from having to do A... B... or C! Think outside the box and put yourself in the shoes of someone who contemplates decisions in an exhaustive fashion before buying... and appeal to that type of person too (not just emotional, impulse buyers).

22. Up-sells, down-sells, backend offers

This can be where the REAL money is made. Front end offers can be where you break even (if you are paying for traffic) and up-sells can be where you turn a profit. Back-end offers can be where you rake it in.

Think about what the up-sell offers will be ahead of time. Is there a way you can offer a premium version of your product? Or, maybe you can add continuity or a paid newsletter of sorts. Perhaps you offer consulting or group webinars. Maybe it's a PLR product you provide or an interview club.

If you want to make a lot more money, then add in up-sells. I like to have 2 or 3 up-sells. To many can be annoying, and some customers hate up-sells. Some complain a lot about up-sells.

But, it's marketing and it works and anytime I see someone complaining about up-sells, I instantly think "they are not a marketer"... they are a customer.

Sure, you want to treat people right and over-deliver, but some things in business... is just business. You are in this to make profits and do good things, but don't let those who express their opinions on up-sells ruin that profit base for you. Believe me, if up-sells did not work, marketers would not be using them and customers would not be buying them!

Here's a quick intro script to get your up-sells going:

(sales video intro script):

Thanks so much for buying _____. You made a wise decision, but do not close this page. This might be the only time you ever see this special one time opportunity. If you click away, this page could be gone forever.

You just purchased _____ and as a special one time offer, I'd like to provide you with an incredible deal. As a special marketing test, I'm prepared to open up the vault and provide you with the following: (list out what they get, then close them)

Up-sells are where big money can come in. If you have an affiliate program set up (you should) then the up-sells can really make your launch. You could give 50% commissions on the front end (or higher) and you can give less on the backend, and many affiliates are fine with that.

Some will never even ask.

The point is, that's where you can make a significant income. These up-sells have to be solid and you need to dial them in for conversions. If needed, continue to change them up, switch out the offers, and make them sell.

If you find yourself paying for traffic, and that traffic is expensive, you are going to have to have up-sells to make that traffic work – most of the time. The front end offer tends to pay for the traffic, and the up-sells is where the profit comes from. This allows you to compete for expensive keywords.

If you see $1 per click traffic and wonder how marketers are affording that much in clicks, now you know. The profits are often found in the backend.

23.   Damaging admission

This is where you admit to something that's actually damaging to your sales pitch on purpose. This increases believability. It makes your offer more trust worthy.

For example:

I am so terrible at technical stuff I can barely tie my shoes... so if an idiot like me can do this, I know you can too!

Condensed Conversion Cheat Sheet:

1. Headline
2. Sub headline
3. Introduction
4. Proof factors
5. Homer Simpson Level
6. Reason why
7. Bullet Points
8. Objections
9. Not for, don't need to
10. Value stacker
11. Price
12. Guarantee
13. Closing statement
14. PS's
15. Contact us
16. Scarcity
17. Know your market best
18. Fears
19. Identity
20. What the market is hot about right now
21. Why is it a smart purchase?
22. Up-sells (sales process)
23. Damaging admission

Step 10

You are going to be doing a lot of testing, tracking and tweaking if you are going to be an effective marketer. Testing is essential to profits. The more you test, the more you dial in your conversions.

The better you convert, the more you make. The more you make, the more you make. It's a snowball effect. As you grow, you grow faster and faster.

If you find yourself tweaking all the time, then you know you are finally in the "game" of marketing. At first, a new marketer, who finds he/she testing a lot, can get frustrated. But, eventually, every successful marketer realizes it's the key to success.

Eventually, the testing becomes part of the game and testing and measuring metrics becomes interesting. It becomes a challenge to dial in the conversions and make it convert better.

There's lots of testing products available online. Prosper202 is one that is pretty popular... many like using Google Optimizer as well. You'll have to find one that works well for you.

Here are the main components to test:

- Your offer
- Your headline
- Your introduction
- Your guarantee
- Your price
- Your bonuses
- Other

There are tons of variables to test... graphics, everything you can think of. However, there is one major thing that can change conversions big time!

If you find your sales page is not converting well, it could be a number of reasons causing it to fail. It could be that nobody wants that product. It could be it's too expensive. It could be the sales copy is terrible. It could be something is turning the customers off. It could be the graphics are terrible. It could be a number of things that's killing conversions.

However, if you have tried dialing in your copy with tweaking and testing all of those things and it still does not convert, there could be one major thing you can do to increase conversions.

That is changing your offer!

Whatever your main offer is... the main presentation... the main USP (unique selling proposition)... whatever your big promise is... your main benefit... that might need to change.

For example, if I'm selling a product on how to make money with Google Adwords, and find my product is not selling, I can change my offer and point of view.

Instead of selling "Google Adwords Techniques" I could change it to "How To Drive Massive Traffic Instantly To Your Site and Convert That Traffic Into Revenue!"

See the difference?

Maybe I'm turning people off by mentioning Google. Maybe it's something else. Maybe it's an ebook, and I should turn it into a "program". Maybe it's a program and I should turn it into a mentoring opportunity. Maybe it's a membership and I should sell a home study course instead.

Maybe I'm providing "Eric's 10 dynamic Steps To Six Figures" and it's not working. So, I change it to "Stacker Formula" and it sells like hot cakes!

Changing up the offer can provide you with huge changes in conversions. It's the number one "conversion factor" other than proof factors!

Proof factors!

If your stuff is not converting, it might be because nobody believes you. Your believability is not working and people are skeptical, and that skepticism is killing conversions.

If I said, "hey, I've made a million dollars online and I'm going to show you how to be a millionaire by next Thursday... and you'll be rich by the end of the month... and we can go swimming in Hawaii this month together and fly around in our huge private airplanes", you might not believe that and not buy.

But, if there are no "proof factors" on your page to back up your claims or big promises, it makes it hard to believe. In fact, since so much of those testimonials are faked, it's great to get video testimonials because they are considered to be real for the most part.

If you get celebrity (or guru) endorsements, that boosts conversions big time. Proof factors are by far one of the main things you need to convert.

When you drive a lot of traffic, and test that traffic, and tweak your stuff to try and convert better and better, you maximize your profits. It can be the difference between NOT MAKING ANY MONEY AT ALL... and making a million dollars per year.

Ask any millionaire marketer about testing and they'll give you a PROFOUND statement that clearly says, "Damn right I test!"

Every single million dollar marketer I know tests and tracks and tweaks!

Step 11

At this point, you know you need to have a squeeze page that captures subscribers onto a list. You need to give away something valuable for free to bribe them into opting in.

Next, you know you need a highly converting salesletter and up-sell process in place and dialed in. You also know you need to test, track and tweak.

We've talked a lot about conversions because it is that important. We've talked about techniques and how to warm up your subscribers to you. We've talked about a lot of stuff for making money thus far.

The clear defining point should be you need to focus most of your time on traffic and conversions. 90% of your time should be spent on traffic and conversions eventually.

In a moment, we will get into traffic... the lifeblood of this business. But, before we do, there's one more thing I want to hit on hard.

And that is...

Pick one business!

Too many marketers fail because they are all over the place, starting all kinds of projects all over the place, all the time. I've written about this already in this report, but think about it one more time...

If you focused on building one business, for the longterm, you'd have tons of backlinks coming in to your site, you'd have your conversions dialed in and popping, you'd have your product keyed up with lots of value, you'd have your squeeze pages rocking, you'd have affiliates selling for you and you'd be growing and growing that business bigger and bigger each and every month.

However, in this business, it's too easy to start up a new project and ignore or forget the last one you were working on. This means all your products are only getting 20% or so of your best effort and focus.

One business you grow and build over time is also a business that grows so big, you can sell it for big bucks eventually perhaps. I urge you to make one business successful, and then expand to others.

However, as an info-marketer, when you master the fundamentals of direct response marketing, you can make a fortune off of what is called, "The moving parade"

The Moving Parade!

At a parade, you see floats passing by, one after another... on to the next shiny, dazzling new float and on and on...

This is how the IM market is. They see a shiny new object in front of them and buy it. Then, they move on to the next shiny new object and so on. They forget what they bought and move on. Many times, they never even download what they bought. Or they skim it and move on to something else. They buy a product, get excited, start skimming it, and then go check their email and forget about it forever after that.

It's a moving parade. It's one product (float) after another. The next thing you know, you look back and you spent a fortune in this market and have not made much money to show for it.

This is very common and happens with thousands of people. No wonder so many are jaded huh?

Well, don't get caught up in the moving parade. Instead focus on this report and follow the steps. Be the one who starts a real business and sticks to it. Be the one who sells products to the "herd" through the moving parade system.

I've had customers who have bought from me for years. Some have spent thousands of dollars with me and they continue to buy again and again. Some take the advice and move on to make themselves a bunch of money.

Others never get anywhere... because they cannot get out from behind the moving parade. They cannot stop buying... and start doing. You are either a seller... or a buyer. Sure, we all buy stuff... but you are either primarily a seller or a buyer. If you are a buyer, then you could be stuck in the moving parade. If you've been at this for a long time and still not making money, then you are in the parade and need to stop that and focus on one business and make that one business work...

However, if you get into certain niche markets, you can certainly earn a fortune by selling stuff in that moving parade mechanism or system or whatever you want to call it.

For example, I can come out with a new product every week and sell it to my lists and every week I'll make money. It's a moving parade and if you sell in that parade (launch and sell a lot of stuff) you can make a fortune.

So, although I say you should stick to one business and make it work... I mean that, but after you have your first launch and make that first business work, you might find yourself also in the moving parade again, but this time as a seller!

You're now the floats.

(or something like that)

Any way you slice it, it's a very valuable insight and you should be saying "thank you Eric" right about now. ☺

The Best DAMN Traffic Report You Are Likely To Find... Evah'

Also, Again By Eric Louviere

Without traffic, life is a frozen field. If you have no traffic, it's like being a bird that cannot fly. It is a sad and lonely world without abundant traffic.

If you are not making money online, it is because, you are not driving traffic. The real question to ask yourself is, when are you going to drive more traffic?

If that answer is "Right now!"

Then, I give you permission to continue reading the rest of this report. And, I give you ample permission to send me testimonials here:

http://ericlouviere.com/helpdesk/

Shall we begin?

To Get Traffic Is To Be Focused!

It's simple really. Those who do not get traffic are just not focused enough on one thing. They are jumping around from one thing to the next, chalking up excuses for not making money yet, but the biggest reason I have found is they are not focused on one thing!

Seriously. If this comes across sort of brutal, it's because it's true. The only people who have an excuse for this is the newbies... the brand new people who are yet to even have a clue what they are doing, much less focusing on one thing.

And if you are one of them that's new like that, then you are one lucky individual to have found this report so early in your career. I urge you to focus on this report and just ignore the heck out of everything else. If there's something in this report you need clarification on or to expand on, then research only that one thing until you know it like the back of your hand, but ignore all the crap out there and all the shiny new objects.

However, I do need to tell you that you will not make money and you will not get abundant traffic without "focus". It just does not happen. And, if you are not focused and you do drive some traffic, it will be a waste of money most of the time, because it's likely your conversions are not dialed in yet. Focus on TRAFFIC AND CONVERSIONS. That is IT!

Pay for Traffic Or Free Traffic!

You got two choices... pay for traffic or get free traffic. Free might sound like a no brainer, but free = manual labor. There's just no other way. You are either going to work hard for traffic... or you are going to pay for traffic and also work hard for it.

It breaks down like this:

Free traffic = work very very hard for traffic, but you don't spend much at all.

Paid traffic = not as much work, but still some work, but you spend money on it.

So, maybe you are saying you'd still rather get free traffic instead of paying for it. Ok, consider this:

You might need to wait months for that free traffic to actually show up and make a financial dent in your bank account. Paid traffic can start hitting your site in the next hour.

Most people in this business (especially those who are new) just don't have long term thinking... and that delay in gratification (results) can crush their focus. Remember, traffic requires focus.

If months pass by and you have grown tired of this, and are not getting results, it's easy to quit and move on to the next shiny object. However, if you drive traffic via paid traffic, you can start dialing in your conversions right away!

I'm convinced... most people fail at this business because of traffic and conversions. They are terrible at conversions and they can't get traffic. That's it.

So, that means, all you have to do is get good at both and the sky is really the limit. There are so many ways (avenues) to generate traffic that it gets very confusing fast.

I recommend you pick one way of driving traffic that meets you best, and stick to it and make it work. Then, later, after you've made one traffic method work, add another method (avenue) of getting traffic.

We are going to go through different forms of getting traffic, but you need to pick one and stick to it. I'm going to start with the traffic methods that have made me a ton of money over the years and then go to other methods of getting traffic.

This is as real as it's going to get. I'm not sugarcoating this next section at all. I'm going to tell it like it is and let you be the judge. Ready?

JV Affiliates!

By far... and I mean WAY BY FAR... the most amount of money I've made in my entire life thus far has been a direct result of getting joint venture affiliates to promote my products.

I did mention "by far" right?

It is by far the number one way I have brought in over a million online and it's by far the number one way 80% of the marketers I know have too.

Sure, there's paid traffic and SEO and all sorts of ways marketers drive traffic and make money, but it's no joke that getting affiliates to promote for you is the most popular way I've seen.

The challenge newbies or intermediate marketers have to overcome is where to start? How to get affiliates to promote if you don't have a name in the market, don't have a list to reciprocate with, no leverage or assets in the market, etc etc.

That's the biggest challenge for most.

The other biggest challenge is most marketers don't understand the game of getting people to promote for you. They don't like asking people to promote for them and they easily give up when people say no... or don't respond.

The way to beat this challenge is to build leverage for yourself. You need something going for you, something attractive to these other people who can promote for you.

Look, if you want to make the big bucks, you need to be in a market where there's lots of competition, because those are the markets where the big money is being made and those are the markets where you can get a bunch of JV affiliates to promote for you.

Markets such as:

Internet Marketing (make money online)
Real estate investing
Dating/Seduction
Forex and trading
Self Improvement
Big hobbies, like Golf

If your niche market is outside these kinds of markets listed above (big markets like these) then JV affiliates can still work too, and they certainly don't require as much leverage because those other markets are not too savvy with the "direct marketing fundamentals".

In other words, those other smaller markets or non-rabid markets contain businesses that are not savvy about up-sells, conversions, traffic, or even setting up affiliate programs... so it's easier to strike deals with them.

However, in the bigger markets, you have to come to the table with leverage. Here are the forms of leverage you can build/grow and have:

- Ability to drive a lot of traffic (a list for example)
- Ability to convert (copywriting, etc)
- A name in the market and a following
- Association with someone else who can do the above
- Contacts (see association)
- Hot product that sells (conversions)
- A good speaker, presenter, product creator
- Superior technical skills
- Other

You have to build leverage. Any serious marketer will pay attention to you and respond to you, if you can drive them traffic. I once emailed a big star who is very well known in the USA and asked if we could strike a deal where I promoted his online products.

I got his assistant, but then blew it off. Later, the star emailed back directly. Everyone wants more money and cash flow and if you can help them get more cash easily, they are interested.

Therefore, your ability to drive traffic for others is an automatic foot in the door... and then the snowball can roll from there for you. Here's an example of a breakdown of how it can go for a newbie who goes from zero to a six figure online business in the Internet Marketing market.

Breakdown of newbie marketer we'll call Mike:

- Mike sets up a squeeze page giving away a free tool he got created for $100. The tool makes it easy for anyone to create beautiful banners themselves without graphic art skills.
- Mike gives away the tool for free in exchange for opting in to his list and getting his free newsletter.
- He's giving away the tool and he's providing a free newsletter in exchange for subscribers
- Mike then goes and runs an a special offer on the Warrior Forum or other IM forums. He pays $40 to $120 rerunning the ad.
- He gets 2,000 subscribers who are all interested in Internet Marketing
- He then takes those 2,000 subscribers and does list swaps with other marketers (not gurus with big names but other intermediate marketers who have lists)
- Mike sends an email to his list promoting Bob's free offer. Bob gets 700 leads from Mike. Bob's list now grew by a new 700 people.
- Bob promotes Mike's free offer (squeeze page giving away that graphic tool) and Mike now gets an extra 1200 new people on his list. It's now 3,200 on his list.
- Mike lands another list swap with Susan. Mike adds another 500 leads to his list.
- Mike promotes a simple but valuable offer to his list and earns $1,500 in commissions.
- Mike runs another special offer and runs some paid advertising (banners) and adds another 3,000 people to his list... doubling it!
- He's now at around 7,000 leads and they are all pretty fresh leads
- Mike gives them some content for free and sends them a video that brands him better with his list. He also gives them a new free tool as well. They are loving him. They know he lives in Colorado and he loves hiking and fishing. They know he's a laid back guy but a bit funny at times.
- Mike then creates an info product explaining how he built a list of 10,000 people in less than 2 months
- He puts it on click bank

- He also adds an up-sell to a new tool he's created and another up-sell to a mentoring program he's started.
- Mike then goes out and puts his launch on http://www.jvnotifypro.com/
- He starts recruiting people himself too. He goes back to Bob and Susan. He hits up people he's bought products from and people he has a relationship with in the market.
- He runs an ad on the Warrior Forum for JV affiliates to sign up to his launch
- He gets a list of JV affiliates to target and starts emailing them.
- He crafts a killer JV email asking these people to promote and promises to return the favor and promote for them too.
- Mike gets 20 people to agree to promote his new product.
- Mike launches his product and 12 of the 20 promote and the others give him excuses (they are slammed busy with other stuff).
- The one's who give him excuses, he gets them to schedule a later mailing and nails them down on a schedule to commit to. All 8 agree to promote later.
- Mike does $40,000 on his launch and 20k goes to affiliates. So, he only made 20k.
- Not bad, but not six figures.
- However, Mike now has really increased his list. He now has 25,000 people on his list and a lot of new customers too.
- Mike starts promoting other marketer's products as an affiliate and starts earning $10,000 to $15,000 per month in affiliate commissions.
- Mike is making six figures from his list now
- Mike then creates his next product five months later.
- Mike gets 50 people to promote this time and they hit it hard too, because it's converting.
- Mike's second launch does $400,000!
- Mike is now set and has plenty of assets and leverage and is making a fortune online from home. His list is solid because he gives them good quality stuff from time to time and mixes in good solid affiliate offers – earning him commissions.
- Mike started from nothing. He's now making big bucks.

You could be like Mike.

You can set up your product on ClickBank.com and marketers like that, because they know they are going to get paid their commissions. Or, you can set up your own affiliate program with programs like Idevaffiliate.com or 1shoppingcart.com or others.

With those programs, you have to pay the affiliates, which can be a hassle. However, you also don't have to wait on clickbank.com checks either. I recommend going Clickbank.com first though, when first starting out.

Here's a checklist and pointers for recruiting affiliates and doing launches like this:

- Get banners created for them so they can use the banners on their blogs and such
- Do most, if not all, of the work for them.
- Write up swipe email for them so they can just hit send
- Follow up is KEY! Don't just ask once and move on. You have to sell them and close affiliates and follow up. They are all busy and they are used to ignoring people (ignoring emails). Stay on them and keep the carrot in front of them of you returning the favor
- Use names, drop names (I got all these people on board already)
- Keep a spreadsheet and track where you are with each affiliate, what they said and if they agreed to promote or not
- If someone agrees to promote, make sure and keep them to their word
- Affiliates care about EPC (earning per click). Track that and provide it to them. Make sure and split test your salesletter and sales videos and variables to increase EPC. Track conversions and do your best to increase conversions.
- Get your affiliates on to a list. This is an affiliate list and you email them separately from your normal list. You email them encouraging them to email and promote.
- Contests are great for spurring on promotion. Use a leader board and email your affiliates who's winning the promo contest. Affiliates love recognition and they are a bit competitive to beat their peers.
- Try to get each affiliate to mail at least 4 times. If conversions are good, it will not be that big of a challenge to get them to continue

emailing. But if conversions are not good, it could be a done deal after the first or second email promotion they do for you

- Give the JV affiliates (who have lists) the product free
- Get testimonials from them if it does well. Use those testimonials for future launches to recruit other affiliates
- If needed, hire a JV manager to recruit affiliates for you, give them a percentage. The good ones tend to want an upfront investment too in their services, and it can be WELL worth the investment too. They can turn a simple $50k launch into a 1 million dollar launch!
- Copy, Conversions, conversions and more conversions! You need to dial that in and make sure you've got a good salesletter or a good sales video and that it's very good and very compelling. That's where the big money is made!
- Webinars can be a great way to get affiliates to promote. You schedule a live webinar and get the affiliates to promote that webinar registration page. All the people your affiliates refer, get cookied to their affiliate link. Then, at the end of the webinar, sell them on your product and close them on the call. This is an event and it can convert great if done right. (more on this later in the report)
- Test your up-sells, and do your best to get those to convert.
- Constantly communicate with your affiliates. Since they are on a list, email them every day reminding them it's launch time, about the leader board, about the stats, pushing them to promote again, etc.
- Personal emails work best. Phone is better. Skype is good too. Instead of only sending broadcast emails out to your JV affiliate list, try emailing some of your affiliates individually and hit them up to promote. If you have phone numbers, call them. They cannot ignore a phone call like they can an email. Text them. Skype them. Constant communication and "asking" is the key. Just get really good at asking for stuff.
- Integration. Some affiliates might ask you if they can integrate their offers in your download pages or members area. I like to put those bonuses under "bonus" content... so it's separate from my content. This is a smart move on your affiliates end to ask for this integration. You should do the same with others. See if you can get your products or squeeze offers into other people's launches to get free buyer leads.

A couple years ago, I had a meeting in my office. I asked a few of my best staff members to set me up with webinars each and every week. Someone was going to be my JV manager and go out there and schedule, plan and organize weekly webinars.

On these webinars, I would give good content to the attendees, but also pitch our coaching program offer at the end of the call. My JV mgr job would be to reach out to other marketers and schedule these webinars with them.

This is how it would break down:

- Bob agrees to promote my killer webinar so he can make big bucks as an affiliate
- Bob gets an affiliate link and swipe JV email copy we created for him, and he mails his lists telling them to register for a free webinar.
- His list clicks his affiliate link and goes to a registration page (for the webinar I'm doing).
- All those people who register are now cookied to Bob's affiliate ID. If they buy anything from me, he gets commissions.
- However, I'm also building a bigger list. All those people who register for the webinar are simultaneously opted into my Aweber list (single opt in)
- There are scripts that do this BTW
- Next, I remind the subscribers about the webinar coming up via emails. Plus, the webinar platform reminds them too (I use gotowebinar.com for this)
- Then, I do the webinar. On the webinar, I give them good content that is valuable and helps them. At the end of the call, I pitch them on my program (or product). I tell them to go to WHATEVER.com to buy the special deal.
- The people on the call rush to buy, and Bob (and me) make money. Plus, I built a bigger list!
- Wash, rinse and repeat with other JV affiliates.

- Sure, you can record the webinar once and replay it, but I'm yet to find a quality platform for playing back the recording. We usually just put the recording up on a page, with a buy now button below the video and continue emailing about getting the program. They can watch the replay.
- Most sales should come from the promotion of the replay. This includes Bob continuing to email about the replay too. Bob will do so, and continue to mail about the replay if he is making good money and its converting (again, it's all about conversions!)

This is a fantastic way to build a business, build a list, build assets, make money, brand yourself in the market, and much more!

Instead of trying to pull off a huge million dollar launch in a week or a day, you can do rolling launches like this or a webinar rolling launch and still do a million (just not in a day).

I have some close marketing buddies who's main (entire) business and cash flow is what I just covered with you... and they do several hundreds of thousands per year!

It works.

However, you have to be willing to get in front of people and speak, conduct webinars and close the deals. That's not for everyone. If it's not for you, but you still want to follow this formula, consider finding someone who is good at that and partner with them. Cater to your own strengths and cater to other people's strengths.

In other words, let them do what they do best and you do what you do best! But, I still think it's just a matter of getting outside yourself and doing things that are a bit nerve racking. I used to feel nervous speaking in front of large groups of people... but after the 1,000th time doing so, I'm no longer nervous at all. I escaped that comfort zone and now it's quite comfortable for me to do webinars.

If you want more money, you need to grow and progress as a business person and individual. If that desire for wealth is strong enough, you'll do webinars or anything else to achieve your goals. It's a great feeling too... to do stuff that used to be outside your comfort zone. It just takes focus. ALL OF THIS JUST TAKES FOCUS.

Whatever you focus on expands!

Webinar Cheat Sheet!

- Introduction: Introduce yourself, be excited and enthusiastic, make the call seem loaded and pumped with high activity. (I'm already seeing tons of questions coming in... lots of people on the call tonight... this is exciting... I see some familiar faces on the attendee list...etc)
- Drop a hook (I'm going to give you a special gift at the end of this call, so you'll want to get that!)
- Practice the slide show ahead of time, record it and watch your recording while taking notes to improve your presentation. Know the material well, know the slides very well and have fun.
- If you are a little nervous, realize they cannot tell.
- When you start the presentation, ignore the question panel or the attendees in the room and focus on your presentation. They can throw you off if you read their questions and it's not going to be a good presentation for the rest of the attendees
- Use the word "you" a lot in your presentation instead of "all of you". For example, "you are going to be able to use this to earn more money" instead of "all of you are going to be able to use this..."
- Give good content at the beginning of the call. Turn them on to you. Teach them stuff. Forget about making money or thinking about money, focus on value. Focus on helping people and the money will come!
- Make it fast moving. Your presentation needs to be high tempo and engaging. You are not going to be able to teach the entire concept or product in one call, so don't try to. Give them nuggets of good quality information and move on to the next slides.

- Answering questions at the end of the call can kill the sale sometimes. It gets people thinking of objections they might not have been thinking of. But because you answered someone's question on "how much time is this going to take me to follow this" now they are all thinking the same thing.
- Think about the objections or questions people will have ahead of time and include or overcome those objections in your presentation. If you do get a lot of questions, download the question report or get a friend to monitor the questions panel and make sure next time you do a presentation, you cover those questions as part of your pitch and presentation. It's valuable information you can use, but answering those questions is hard to pull off and still make sales.
- Follow all the "conversion" fundamentals in this report, on your pitch (Big promise, special deal, urgency and scarcity, solid guarantee, etc etc)
- Close them strong!
- Be enthusiastic!
- Tell them their problems are answered and their desires are fulfilled by buying right now, and to *not buy* will result in further frustration and agitation with the same problems.
- After you close strong, end the call and tell them you'll see them inside the program.
- Your presentation (webinar) is like one big sales letter. It starts out with some content though and it hits on the same triggers as a salesletter does. Proof factors, credibility, celebrity, authority, social proof, etc etc...

Sales flow:

- Introduction, build credibility and set the tone for the rest of the call.
- Drop a hook (I have a gift for you at the end of this call)
- Enthusiastic (be excited about the information being revealed and the call)
- State the problems people have
- You have the solution
- why you decided to create this product

- you found how awesome it worked (proof)
- you let friends use it too and it worked great for them (proof)
- you then let even others use it and word got around, people came to you and it worked for them too (proof)
- anyone can use it (damaging admission, if I can do it, you can do it...)
- anyone can do this, hammer that home
- proof
- proof
- proof
- social proof
- Transition to pitch (what you get)
- Bonus
- special price
- guarantee
- scarcity
- closing statement (if you want a ton of traffic very easily, get this)
- gift
- closing statement again (if you are sick and tired of not getting enough traffic or making money, get this product)
- call to action (go now!)
- end call

Paid Traffic!

By far, JV affiliates has been the biggest income maker I've ever done before... but after that, in second place, is paid traffic.

And, just like me, it's the same for most marketers I know too. In fact, for every marketer I really-really know, there's only a few who generate six figures using free traffic methods (besides JV affiliates) and the overwhelming majority of six figure marketers get their traffic from:

1. JV Affiliates
2. Paid Traffic

Now, if you look at those two ways to drive traffic... and keep in mind that about 97% of the marketers out there who earn six figures ALSO do so by these two forms of getting traffic... it becomes obviously clear, how to drive traffic.

Unfortunately, most marketers who don't make money ignore #1 and #2 from above. Most marketers focus on "free traffic" from writing articles and whatnot.

Now, that works too... but in my opinion... in professional, expert, million dollar opinion, writing articles and whatnot should be a secondary traffic method to the two above.

Yes, writing articles works... and if you want to make a few hundred dollars per month for a long while, then go for it. But, if you want to make six figures or create a solid income --- the kind you can quit your day job with --- then you'll focus on #1 or #2 above (if not both!)

That does not mean you cannot do article marketing, SEO, etc too. You can, but I would advise nailing down and mastering the two above. It will make you a far better marketer and will make all those free traffic methods work that much better.

You don't have to spend a fortune on paid traffic either. You can start very small and very cheap. In fact, I recommend you start cheap and small, so you can dial in your conversions.

I can guarantee you, you will not hit a grand-slam home run with conversions right out of the gate. You are going to have to tweak your conversions and paid traffic to make it work.

Ok, enough twisting your arm to do JV Affiliates and Paid Traffic... let's get into what to do and how to do it.

Paid Traffic Can Be FREE!

If you knew for certain your salespage converts, you'd send paid traffic from all over the net! Let's go through a breakdown:

- Mike puts $50 in Facebook Advertising to drive paid traffic
- He also puts $50 into PlentyOfFish.com to drive paid traffic
- That is $100 he's going to spend on traffic
- He drives that traffic and spends up the $100 in a week
- He got some subscribers on his list, but only made $50 in sales
- He lost $50 on the campaign.
- Mike quits and goes to article marketing

But Bob sticks to it and tweaks his stuff.

- Bob puts another $100 into Facebook, because it worked better than Plenty Of Fish
- But this time, he bids on less keywords
- He tweaks his squeeze page
- Instead of having sales copy, he adds a sales video
- He adds some professional graphics
- He tries it this time and makes $100
- He broke even, did not lose money but did not make money
- But, it's better than last round.
- Bob breaks out this book here because he bought it and loves it very much and thinks this book is the best damn thing since sliced bread, so he opens it up again and reviews the portion on conversions.
- Bob realizes he must warm up his new subscribers and realizes they are very-very skeptical to buy from him.
- He creates a free report and sends it to his list. Inside the free report is a link back to his product (pitching them again) and what do you know... 5 people buy!
- He sends another email saying "in case you missed my last email, here's the free report again. People are loving it!" and this time he makes 12 sales!

- He then fires up Facebook Advertising again and deposits another $100!
- BUT, he also adds that free report to his auto-responder email sequences so all his traffic gets that report right away (instantly when they opt in).
- This time he spent $100, but he made $225!
- He made a profit of $125!
- He puts in another $100 and this time he makes $175 (a little less but still profit)
- He then fires up POF again, because he's tweaked his stuff since the first time and BAM! He makes $50 in profits
- Now, he's averaging between $150 to $225 per day of profits!\
- All because he did what?

He
Did
Not
Quit

And, he focused on conversions. He focused on tweaking and testing. He stuck to one thing. He did not quit and then move on to something else.

This is the name of the game with paid traffic. And, once you have a winning campaign and see that money coming in (profits)... you'll never look back. Articles and social networking stuff will be Childs play to this kind of profits.

Paid Traffic Platforms

Facebook is a platform for getting paid traffic driven to your site. Facebook has gone through a lot of changes, but is quickly becoming a great place to drive traffic through.

One thing that's important though, it at the time of writing this, you have to figure out exactly how Facebook likes your landing pages. The two step approach (talked about earlier in the report) works a little better.

You see, Facebook, for some reason, does not want to abuse their users. They are picky. It's like they want you to spend money advertising, but not sell anything.

So, you have to get a bit creative.

You create a landing page that is a survey or asks questions, gets the visitor interactive... give them content for free... then have them opt in to get more information.

Here's an example of a page taken straight from Facebook Advertising:

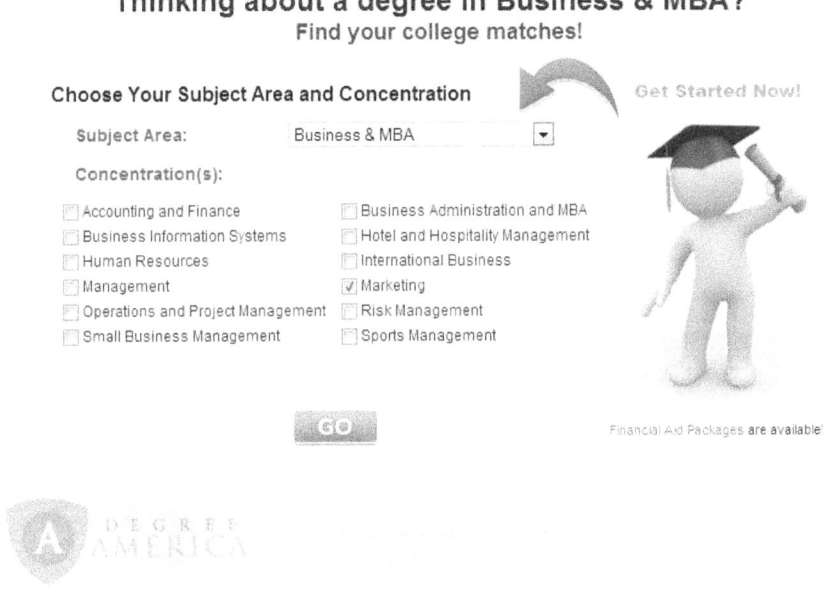

Notice above how this page is not a traditional squeeze page, but it's a form they need to fill out and click "go". This engages the visitors into getting involved in the page (form)

Next, after you click "Go", here's the next page you see:

Which **Business & MBA** Program Suits Your Needs?

Find out now in less than 3 minutes!

PROGRESS [_____]

How old are you?

| Please select one | ▾ |

Next Steps

• Fill out our easy-to-complete form

• We will match you with up to three custom schools

• Receive free educational consultations and learn more about the financial aid options available to you!

FACT:

Students who request information from three or more universities make better decisions than their peers who do not. Weigh your options and make the right choice!

DEGREE
AMERICA

The second page is another form or answer to give. Then another one, and then another one and so on... Then finally, it asks you to enter your zip code and email address.

See the final page below:

Which **Business & MBA** Program Suits Your Needs?
Find out now in less than 3 minutes!

« Back PROGRESS

What is your postal code?

What is your email address?

Continue

Next Steps
• Fill out our easy-to-complete form

• We will match you with up to three custom schools

• Receive free educational consultations and learn more about the financial aid options available to you!

FACT:
Students who request information from three or more universities make better decisions than their peers who do not. Weigh your options and make the right choice!

DEGREE
AMERICA

As you can see above, that's when they get the opt in. This was straight from Facebook and they followed what Facebook wants. This one is more like a five or six step form and then they ask for the opt in.

So, it makes it a bit harder to get the subscribers, but those subscribers you do get will be more qualified and more motivated usually.

Therefore, all you really need to do is find what people want and then give it to them, then sell them all the other things they are interested in.

Always market to "demographics"... If you give someone a free report on losing weight, what else will they be interested in?

Organic foods
Yoga
Energy
Self improvement
Beauty stuff

Karate
Strength training
Rock hard abs
Buns of steel

See what I mean? The key is to capture subscribers and then turn them on to YOU. Then, sell them other stuff they are already buying and are interested in.

Plentyoffish.com is a bit like facebook is for advertising. It's a growing site and it's a dating or socializing site, so you can reach people based on their interests.

These users fill out their profiles and tell you a lot. If they are into Yoga, they usually put that on their profiles... and you can target them based on those keywords. It's pretty slick.

Google Adwords, Yahoo, MSN, Bing, etc are all Pay Per click formats too, but they are all going through crazy changes and are a bit ridiculous at the moment in my opinion.

I used to bank on Google Adwords so much it's crazy... but Adwords is banning most marketers and for no reason. If you market a "make money" product on Adwords, they are quick to ban.

I've also heard if they had any problems collecting payments from you, you are instantly banned too. Also, to really get good results from Adwords you'll have to have a high quality score.

That means you'll have to SEO your site... have meta tags... a site map... terms and conditions... an address... a phone number... alt text links... link backs and so on.

It's almost better to go for SEO and rankings on Google nowadays than it is to pay for ads. Google had changed their algorithms so that backlinks are very important again. That's helping savvy marketers rank high, especially for long-tail keywords.

Banners!

Banners have always been a great way for getting traffic. Again, it is going to take tweaking and testing. It's going to take focus. That's all that is standing in the way between you and a lot more money.

Basically, all you'd have to do is find sites that offer advertising in your niche and contact them about advertising there. You could use Google Ad Planner, and search your main category and find sites that accept text ads or image ads.

If they take text ads or image ads, then they should be interested in what you have to offer. Never go for the instant rate card. Whatever rate card they give you, shoot lower.

It's negotiable and many sites just want the cash flow, so they'll take lower than rate card. Negotiate with them. Think ahead of time exactly what you'd like to get and then go get it.

Visualize what you want, accept it in your head that you already got it, then go get it.

Below is a screen shot of Ad Planner.

Site profile   bodybuilding.com

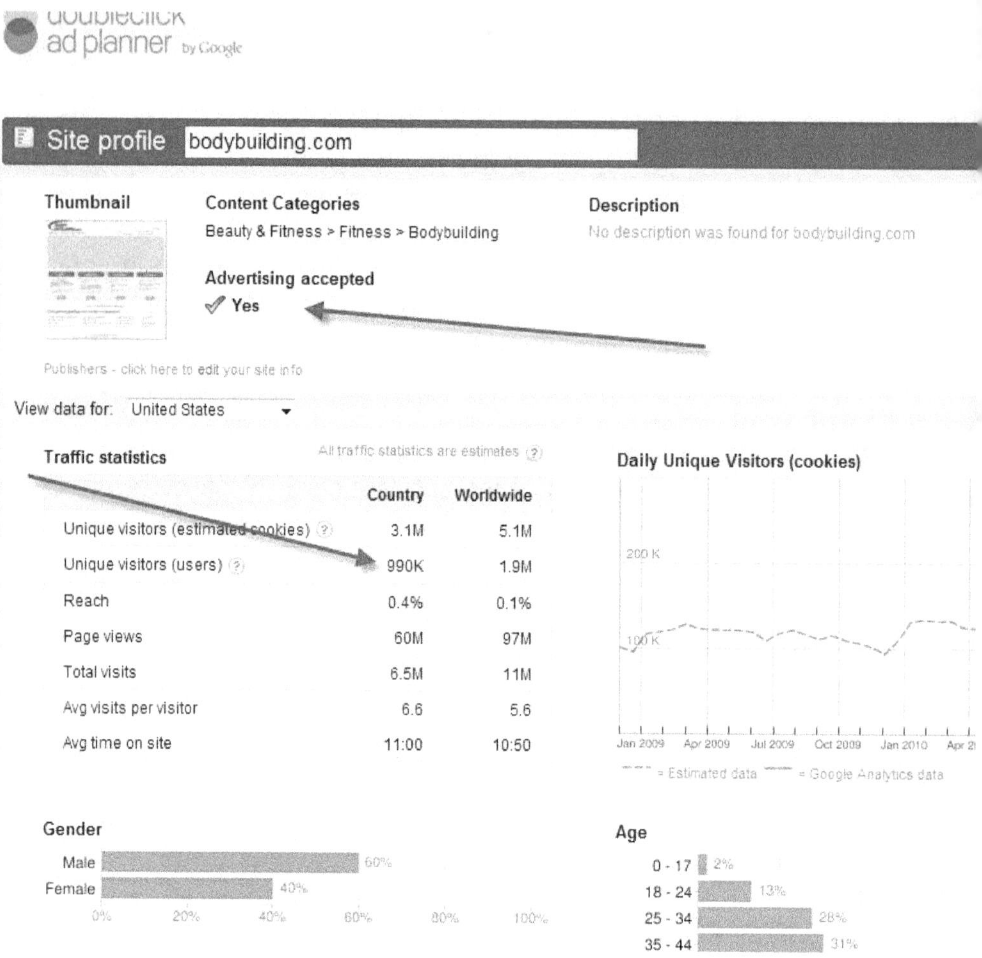

Thumbnail	Content Categories	Description
	Beauty & Fitness > Fitness > Bodybuilding	No description was found for bodybuilding.com

Advertising accepted

✓ Yes ⬅

Publishers - click here to edit your site info

View data for: United States   ▼

Traffic statistics   All traffic statistics are estimates (?)

	Country	Worldwide
Unique visitors (estimated cookies) (?)	3.1M	5.1M
Unique visitors (users) (?)	990K	1.9M
Reach	0.4%	0.1%
Page views	60M	97M
Total visits	6.5M	11M
Avg visits per visitor	6.6	5.6
Avg time on site	11:00	10:50

Daily Unique Visitors (cookies)

200 K

100 K

Jan 2009   Apr 2009   Jul 2009   Oct 2009   Jan 2010   Apr 20

--- = Estimated data   ──── = Google Analytics data

Gender

Male ▓▓▓▓▓▓▓ 60%
Female ▓▓▓▓▓ 40%

0%   20%   40%   60%   80%   100%

Age

0 - 17 ▓ 2%
18 - 24 ▓▓▓ 13%
25 - 34 ▓▓▓▓▓▓ 28%
35 - 44 ▓▓▓▓▓▓▓ 31%

Notice at top, the red arrow is pointing to "YES" they accept advertising. Also, notice they get tons of clicks and unique visitors. All you have to do is contact them. This example is for "body building" and the site I pulled up is bodybuilding.com

If you were in the weight loss or fitness or body building niche, this could be a great find depending on costs.

First go for Pay Per Click and figure out your conversions. Figure out your metrics and then go for cost per view. See if you can **A)** get your traffic cheaper and **B)** increase your conversions.

That's marketing. That's business. This is how it works. This is how the big boys play. This is what it takes to get up there in income. You can start small and grow it and before you know it, you're rolling.

Again, what is this... the five thousandth time I've said this... "It's all about traffic and conversions!"

Everything Else When It Comes To Traffic!

Look, traffic is a big giant topic. It's ever changing too. It's never static and always dynamic. What worked a few months ago, might not work a few months from now.

However, what never changes... is the basic fundamentals of direct response marketing. People are people, marketers are marketers and customers will continue to buy information.

Mastering advertising and media buys, and conversions, can make you wealthy for a long time to come. Heck, even if the Internet exploded and did not exist anymore, with these skills, you could make a fortune in direct mail or offline marketing.

Beyond what's been explained already for traffic, here are some other ways to get traffic:

- Video marketing (using Youtube and other video sites).
- Article marketing
- Local marketing using Google Local, Yahoo local, etc
- Direct Mail (see nextmark.com)
- SEO
- Integration with other sites
- Cross promoting
- Ezine and solo ads

- List swaps
- Classified ads
- Banners
- Social networking
- Using free software giveaways
- Using free software downloads
- PPC Mgmt
- And more

However, one last time... the best and biggest money I've ever made has come from JV Affiliates and Paid Traffic, period.

Focus On Your Strengths, Outsource Your Weaknesses!
Outsourcing Exposed!

One of the biggest breakthroughs I ever had was figuring out what my strengths and weaknesses were. Some things were in the gray area between strengths and weaknesses, but for the most part, I knew what I was good at and what I was terrible at.

I was terrible at: technical stuff and I was terrible at managing people

Therefore, I outsourced that stuff... or I partnered with people who would take care of that for me. For the longest time, I spun my wheels getting nowhere.

And, if I did finish something, it took a very long time.

I learned about speed bumps and I heard this saying from a mentor of mine: "money loves speed!"

Well, if money loves speed, then money hates speed bumps. Speed bumps slow you down, and sometimes for years!

You have to decide what you are good at and what you enjoy. Figure out what you gravitate towards. We are not good at everything. We tend to be good at certain things.

Remember the four main categories:

1. Traffic
2. Conversions
3. Product Creation
4. Technology

Which are you strong at? Are there any that stand out to you, or that you are most interested in? Where are you weak? Well, let's say you are strong at product creation but weak at traffic.

Then, focus on product creation and get someone else to do the traffic. Partner with someone strong at traffic. It's likely someone who is strong at traffic does not like to create products.

It's also likely that anyone strong at traffic DOES NOT WANT TO SPEND TIME CREATING PRODUCTS EITHER.

Let me say this again loudly:

> ***You Cannot Possibly Create Products Fast Enough To Meet The Buying Demands Of Your Subscribers And Customers And Marketplace!***

That means even those marketers who have lists and can drive a lot of traffic, still need products. AND, they prefer products that have their own names on them. So, instead of promoting affiliate offer after affiliate offer, they can simply focus on traffic, while you focused on creating products. It's a good match.

Or, maybe you are not good at anything but product creation so far. Others can cover that by either partnering with you, or by you paying someone to do it for you.

There's no need to partner with a webmaster who only takes 20 minutes to set up your site. You can pay that person $50 or so and be done with it.

The big two are: Traffic & Conversions.

If you are not strong at those two, you need to get strong at one of them, at least. And, if you're not strong at those two, you need to be very strong at Product Creation (very strong).

Paying People To Do Stuff For You

The big one is copywriting. That is a big expense. It's gotten cheaper over the years because of video sales letters. More marketers are doing video letters and not paying copywriters to write long letters for them.

This is fine, and if you can pull off a compelling sales video, go for it. Otherwise, paying someone to write copy can be expensive. So, I recommend either forking out the investment for a high quality copywriter, or starting with a junior copywriter.

I tell my 1-on-1 VIP clients to start with writing it themselves (it's great practice and it is time well spent). Then, get a junior copywriter to rewrite it or tweak it. That's cheaper for you. It all depends on your budget.

The next big one is technical. This is where a lot of newbies spin their wheels for a long time. I did. Basically, you have to bite the bullet and fork over some cheap money to get stuff done for you if you are not good at it yourself.

You can simply go to Craigslist.org and run ads for webmasters. They are everywhere. You can also go to Craigslist.org and click on the country Philippians and run an ad targeting them. They are much cheaper and good people who work hard. They can be very loyal to you as well and do you well.

I'd make sure and get this taken care of for you:

- **Squeeze page**
- **Front end offer**
- **Payment processing**
- **Up-sell**
- **2nd Up-sell**
- **3rd Up-sell**
- **Protected download area**
- **Affiliate program**
- **Etc.**

Get those things covered and you are good to go. Maybe throw in getting a blog set up with WordPress and then you can spend all your time focused on the most important things (traffic & conversions).

One of the techniques I have used it to hire two people to do the same thing. Then, I quickly fire the one who is not communicating with me constantly and who is not doing a good job, and keep the other one.

It's business.

But, I've wasted so much money over the years being a nice guy and paying people to sit around and do nothing that I've earned the right to split test human beings. ☺

There's no real trick to outsourcing, but I'd say the main thing you should do is stay on top of that person you are paying and have high expectations and hold them to that.

It's easy for them to slack off because they do not see you all day every day. You are just some person on the net sending them money. They can be playing video games all day instead of doing what you are paying them to do.

The Best DAMN Wealth Mindset Book To Infinity And Beyond!

Also, Again, of course, it's By Eric Louviere

If you would like to be very wealthy, then you'll read every word that follows. If you want a lot of money in your life, then you'll read the rest of this with an open mind and put all the preconceived notions you have and follow along and absorb what's being said and revealed here.

We all have beliefs, religions, whatever you want to label it, but what follows works, period. However, it's not something to just read and cast aside.

Have you ever read "Think And Grow Rich"? Have you ever read "The Science of Getting Rich"? Have you read countless other books on wealth? Chances are you might have.

But have you ever studied those books? I mean really studied them? If you believe they are true and they work, and what's written in those books is real, then have you ever really studied them?

Have you tried applying what's taught in them? Have you memorized some of the principles and learned them so well, you know them by heart?

I have found, in my career, that most super successful people follow those laws to a certain point. I'm not really going hokey on you or mystical here, I'm just saying that even if you take those principles and apply them in a practical manner (non super natural), they work!

It's pretty obvious to me after analyzing this stuff for decades. I've paid close attention to the super successful and the very rich. I have picked their brains dry. I have had dinner with a billionaire and I can tell you point blank, there's a difference.

There's a difference between the way they think, act, speak and believe. There's such a stark difference, but it's only noticeable if you know what to look for.

You can cast off what I'm about to say, you can chalk it up as hocus pocus and you can debate me till the cows come home, I'm more than convinced, what I'm about to share with you is the secret to wealth.

The hard part is living it.

The easy part is understanding it and believing in it, the hard part is making the choices to live it daily!

I believe over time, it can become more and more of a habit and part of you. But, there's a huge difference between "lack thinking" and "abundant" thinking.

You may already know that, but do you live it?

Probably the best thing I could ever recommend to anyone, is to read and get the audios to The Science Of Getting Rich. Commit the lessons to memory and listen/read it every single day until you are rich!

There is nothing on this Earth that has changed my finances more than that book and living the principles outlined in it. Perhaps it's because I believe it so. Who knows? Frankly, I don't care. All I know is it worked for me, and with most of the people I know who are successful (or rich) do the same things (regardless if they believe it or have even ever read the book).

I see them saying things and acting in a certain way, and I say to myself, "that's the SOGR".

I've read countless books and many say the same things, and have the same principles. I can regurgitate them here in this report, or I can simply tell you to go get SOGR and commit it to memory.

Know it like the back of your hand.

I'm serious. If I'm offending you, I am not sorry. You bought this to get rich and to earn more money and I can only tell you the truth. Get it and master it.

I know people who are poor, and they think, act and say the exact opposite of what that book teaches. Any time I come across troubles, it's because I have not been living and acting in a certain way. That way is SOGR.

For example, I have learned a ton from a very successful, legendary copywriter who is now retired. I've devoured his stuff. Well, a few years ago, while going through his material, he said, "If you want to hit a home run with your copy, first imagine it in your mind, then do it!"

Whatever outcome you want, first imagine it, expect it, and act, think and speak as if you already have it, and you'll get it! If you don't get it, then be sure and hold the faith that you will get something better, and it happens.

You have to take action and you have to focus on the tasks at hand and do the very best you can with what's in front of you today, while holding strong, the vision of what you want in your mind.

For example, what do you think about most often each day?

Are you thinking of bills all day? Do you catch thoughts of a negative nature pop into your head all day? Have you ever listened to the mental chatter that goes on in your head? You don't have to try and change it, just witness it.

Listen to the thoughts that pop up in your mind. What are they saying? Do you catch yourself worrying about things? Do you catch yourself worrying about health... bills... relationships... jobs... bosses... coworkers... security... bad things?

If so, then I'd bet you have a lot of that going on. One person I know worries about relationships all the time. It's a dominating thought. I never think about that. I'm married and we're happy and I never worry about it. This friend of mine does. Guess what she has problems with? Relationships!

The old saying, "that you resist, persists". The more you focus on something, the more it expands. If you focus on bad things, you get bad things. If you focus on what you want, you get it.

If you think about bills, then bills become a constant problem. If you think thoughts like this:

"I just need an extra $1,000 per month and then I'll be ok"

Guess what? That's all you'll get. Then what? Perhaps you lose your job next. Guess what could be happening? Your losing that job so you can get another job that pays................. an extra $1,000 per month!

But, that's because of your limited thoughts.

If you say and think, " I want to make 30k per month" then that's a different type of perspective than "I just need to get by". It changes everything. It changes your actions.

Instead of working to just get by, you're working to get to a much higher income level and that's inspiring! You are motivated, excited and you are an advancing person.

If you find yourself always talking bad about others, always casting blame to others, always complaining about things, always making excuses for everything, then you are going to continue to get chaos.

If you change that and are always saying good things about people, always praising others, eliminating excuses, sending love in everything you do and all your thoughts, guess what you are going to get?

If you are an advancing person and you are going somewhere good, and you have that aura about you as an advancing person, guess what you are going to get:

Opportunity!

For example, if I'm feeling low and down about things, and I have lots of negative thoughts, I'm going to confide in others and complain about things.

They are going to look at me as going downhill fast, or up the creek without a paddle. If I'm positive and inspired and going somewhere, and am an advancing person... they see opportunity!

They see an advancing person!

See, it's not all mystical hocus pocus, it's practical stuff. I'm not here to preach religion or anything, I'm here to tell you that you must ACT, THINK, SPEAK, WALK, BREATHE, WRITE AND BE a certain way, to get wealthy!

Value!

If you give value in everything you do, great things will happen in your life. Don't believe me? I dare you... triple double dare you... to try it for 4 days.

You want to change your life? Do this!

In everything you do, in every interaction you have, give more value than what's being given to you! Just give!

I'm not saying go down to the block and give away money to beggers. I'm saying if you are talking to a friend, give that friend your attention and help that friend the best you can. Feel love and feel "gratitude" and give that person what you can in value.

If you have a job, give that job more in value than the job is giving you in wages. Give your boss more in value than your boss gives you in recognition, money, promotions, responsibilities, etc.

Over-deliver!

Give more in value!

In your relationship, give more in value and see what happens. See if you can feel the most love and admiration you can for others and show it in your actions and just watch what happens.

Money?

Same thing!

For example, this report. I want to blow you away with value. I want you to keep this report forever. I want it to change your life. I want you to excel and achieve your dreams. I want you to get rich. I want life to be better for you. I want to take all the things I've learned and help others have more life!

I must have more life too! By me living my life to the fullest... by me having more life... I am inspiring others to do the same! If I share with you what I've learned and my beliefs, I have not short changed you on value.

If you ripped this report off somewhere and got it free somehow, you have got more value from me than you have given me in return. That's on you, not me. I'm providing the value and I'm sending out to the universe my intentions of providing more life for ALL!

All in all, the main reason people don't make money in this business is not because of traffic... or business opportunities... or skills... or experience... or charisma... or speaking abilities... or technical abilities... or copywriting abilities... the main reason is they don't think... act... speak...write... or live in a certain way!

I know a marketer who does nothing but pay others. He just pays good people, good money, to do everything for him. He makes a profit off of that and he does a million dollars. What special skills does he have? Outsourcing? Big deal.

I know people who are kids who make six figures in this business. I know people who are handicapped, who came from prison, who worked at fast food joints... and the list of overachievers is a mile long.

Is it because the internet is available to all, or is it because they did things in a certain way? It is not the techniques, or the schemes or the methods or formulas that make people rich... it's the way they think, act and do and live!

Why is it one carpet cleaning company gets rich while another carpet cleaning company goes broke? People who are rich live in the same community as people who are poor. It's not the environment. The environment can help, but it's them. It's the way they think and live.

The best thing you could do is get into the guts of SOGR. It's all there and that book was written in the early 1900's. It's all there, and it's the only book you really need to follow to get rich.

But, it's not going to work if you casually read it. You have to live it. You have to believe it. Even if you believe it in a practical, non supernatural way, it still works.

I got the audios for this on Itunes. It's called "The Wisdom of Wallace Wattles" and it is good. I comprehend much more from those audios than I do from reading the book. But, that's just me.

I try to listen to it every day, even if it's just a chapter. And, if things ever seen hard or stressed, those audios wipe it out instantly for me.

Look, you hired me on this report to tell the truth... to tell you how to make money online and how to get wealthy. I told the truth. I explained what I do and what I have done to earn the money I've earned, which is over 1 million online to date. I've provided step by step instructions and I've given you more value than what you paid for this report.

It's up to you to take it and use it to achieve more life for you and yours. Thank you for sharing this journey with me!

Respectfully,

Eric Louviere

PS – I do provide 1-on-1 mentoring from time to time for ambitious people who want someone to help them get this stuff done faster and better. If you want to shave off years worth of trial and error and get there faster, simply submit a help desk ticket here and request more information about my VIP mentoring program:

http://ericlouviere.com/helpdesk/